GROWING UP IN SLAVERY

SYLVIANE A. DIOUF

THE MILLBROOK PRESS
BROOKFIELD • CONNECTICUT

To my son, Sény Fakaba Kamara,
and to the memory of the children
who grew up in slavery
—Sylviane Anna Diouf

Photographs courtesy of The Valentine Museum: p. 6; Schomburg Center for Research in Black Culture, The New York Public Library: pp. 10 (Photographs and Prints Division, Astor, Lenox and Tilden Foundations), 20; Library of Congress: pp. 13 (USZ62 054026 207373), 50 (USZ62 30800 207373), 55 (USZ62 30960 207373), 64 (B8171 152-A 207373), 84 (USZ62 37791 207373); Sylviane Diouf: p. 16; © Collection of the New-York Historical Society: pp. 31 (#46628), 33 (#39193), 43 (#48163), 45 (top, #50482; bottom, #47843), 53 (#73354), 67 (#48099); Chicago Historical Society: p. 34 (#P&S-1957.0027); The Historic New Orleans Collection: 39; Missouri Historical Society, St. Louis: p. 48; Historic Stagville, Division of Archives and History, N. C. Department of Cultural Resources: p. 57; Hargrett Rare Book and Manuscript Library, University of Georgia Libraries: p. 71; The Metropolitan Museum of Art, Gift of Erving and Joyce Wolfe, 1982, (1982.443.3), Photograph © 1982 The Metropolitan Museum of Art: p. 74; Massachusetts Commandery Military Order of the Loyal Legion and the U. S. Army Military History Institute: pp. 80, 81; Hampton University Archives: p. 82

Diouf, Sylviane A. (Sylviane Anna), 1952-
Growing up in slavery / Sylvaine A. Diouf
p. cm.
Includes bibliographical references and index.
ISBN 0-7613-1763-5 (lib. bdg.)
Summary:Examines what life was like for children who grew up as slaves in the United States, describing the conditions in which they lived, the work they did, how they were educated, and their efforts to obtain freedom.
1. Child slaves—United States—Social conditions—Juvenile literature. 2. Afro-American children—Social conditions—Juvenile literature. 3. Slavery—United States—History—Juvenile literature. 4. Plantation life—United States—History—Juvenile literature. [1.Child slaves. 2. Slavery.] I. Title
E443 .D55 2001   306.3'62'0830973 21   00-038013

Published by The Millbrook Press, Inc.
2 Old New Milford Road
Brookfield, Connecticut 06804
www.millbrookpress.com

Printed in Hong Kong
Copyright © 2001 by Sylviane A. Diouf
All rights reserved
5 4 3 2 1

Contents

Listening to the Children of Slavery

At the close of the Civil War, four million people in the United States were slaves. More than one million were children under the age of sixteen. When slavery was finally abolished on January 31, 1865, the system had endured in the United States for about 235 years. Over that period of time, millions of children, taken away from Africa or born in America, had been forced to live under a barbaric system.

The children who grew up in slavery were denied the most basic human rights, such as freedom, safety, protection from degrading and cruel treatment, compensation for work done, education, equality, and the right to freely move around. They worked for no pay and were property that could be bought, sold, maimed, or killed.

In the eyes of their families, however, they were children like any others, who needed love, protection, happiness, and education. But the enslaved parents had no say in their children's fate. All they could do was give them as much physical and moral comfort as possible, and provide them with skills to help them survive.

Some children of slavery grew up to share their stories with others in various ways. Most, however, chose not to recall the horrors of their childhood.

Armed with these lessons in endurance, the children set out to make the most of their lives. All had to exhibit resiliency and courage in the face of terrible hardships, and some snatched slim opportunities to learn to read and write whenever possible, or ran away to freedom.

The last people who grew up in slavery died in the 1960s. Many did not want to talk about their childhood and, by the same token, many of their descendants did not want to hear about it. As the daughter of former slaves put it:

> Parents didn't tell their children a lot about slavery. They thought it would cripple 'em . . . Mentally! It would harm them and mess up their future hope. [My parents told] me about slavery and I didn't want to hear about that. Some of the things they were saying I didn't want to hear because it didn't sound so good.[1]

Although many people did not share their memories with their loved ones, others left vivid testimonies in several forms. During slavery, some fugitives who had succeeded in reaching the North (where slavery had been abolished) told their stories to abolitionists—men and women who worked to end slavery—who helped turn the stories into autobiographies. Others such as Frederick Douglass and William Wells Brown were already literate when they ran away, and they wrote their autobiographies by themselves. Former slaves, working with abolitionists, gave speeches that were published in books and pamphlets. Enslaved and free men and women wrote letters that have been preserved. People were interviewed by newspapers and magazines once they were safely in the North or Canada. After the Civil War, historians and other scholars conducted interviews of formerly enslaved men and women. In 1863, the American Freedmen's Inquiry Commission, a government agency, collected accounts by slaves and former slaves. And, finally, between 1936 and 1938, the Works Progress Administration, a project of the federal government, recorded 2,194 interviews of men and women who had experienced slavery.

No person alive today can really know what it was like growing up as an enslaved child in the United States, but all these testimonies help form a picture of the kind of existence the children led. These testimonies inform us about the children's family life, the work they did, the food they ate, the way they were dressed, the punishments they received, the relationships they had with white children, the games they played, and the dreams of education and freedom they nurtured.

The children of slavery can still be heard today through the recollections of the adults they became. Their stories help us better understand them, their community, slavery and its legacy, and ultimately, the history of the people of this country.

Chapter One

African Children: From Freedom to Slavery

Ten years after Europeans landed in the Americas in 1492, a full-scale trade in human beings sent between 12 and 20 million African people across the Atlantic Ocean.[1] Two and a half to four million of them were under the age of fifteen.

Before the Africans, Native Americans were the first victims of enslavement in America. However, as the number of native people declined dramatically due to violent conflicts with settlers who seized their land and to European diseases, the colonists sought another source of free labor. They found it in Africa, where they had first sailed in 1444. At the time, the enslavement of Europeans by other Europeans had stopped, and slavery was considered a brutal system of the past. Nevertheless, this ancient and cruel institution was revived to benefit Europeans and the American settlers.

Millions of Africans were removed by force from their homelands. They were transported to the New World to clear the land and work in the gold and silver mines of South

During the slave trade, African families, like this one from Senegal, were in danger of being broken up by kidnappers and slave dealers, who took the children away and brought them to the New World.

America and on the sugar, cotton, rice, and tobacco plantations established all over the Americas and the Caribbean islands by European settlers. The crops produced by the enslaved Africans and their descendants were sold at great profits by the slaveholders. Most of the products were shipped to Europe, where people were eager to consume the newly introduced sugar and tobacco, to use the American cotton to make fabric, and to turn the precious metals into money and jewelry. The labor of the slaves was used to develop the vast American land, to create wealth, and to fill the needs of European and American consumers.

The number of people enslaved all over the Americas for close to four hundred years was the largest in the world history of slavery. African children were caught in the slave trade because they were profitable. They were made to work hard in the New World, even as children, and harder still as adults. Thus, in the course of a lifetime, their labor would bring immense benefits to their owners.

Some of these children were only a few months old and had been shipped away with their mothers. The vast majority, however, arrived alone. They had been children with little worry and with parents to take care of them, but what they had to experience now was beyond anything they could ever have imagined.

What had happened to them? Why and how had their world been disrupted in such a brutal manner?

Kidnapped

Numerous African children were the victims of kidnapping. During the Atlantic slave trade, bands of organized kidnappers roamed the countryside and seized the most vulnerable, usually children, whom they sold to European and American slave traders.

Traveling from one place to another could be dangerous, as young Salih Bilali discovered. Salih was born around 1770 to a wealthy and distinguished family in Mali. Like some African children who would become slaves in America, as a Muslim, Salih spent most of his time in religious school and learned to read and write Arabic. Salih lived in a large town, Kianah, and visited other cities with his parents. To the

African children, big cities offered a constant spectacle: There were craftspeople working in the open, lively markets, and traders from far away bringing exotic products. Some cities, like the renowned Timbuktu, two hundred miles north of Kianah, had numerous schools and libraries of books written in Arabic. Urban children of wealthy families, such as Salih, usually led a comfortable life. But one day, as the twelve-year-old boy was riding his horse back home from the city of Jenne, he was abducted and taken across the Atlantic. The young boy spent the rest of his life enslaved on a Georgia plantation.

Children were seized while playing in the woods or working in the fields, but staying home was certainly no guarantee of safety. In order to protect themselves when the adults went to work, some youngsters would climb trees to look out for possible abductors. However, as the story of Olaudah Equiano illustrates, things could still go terribly wrong.

Olaudah was an eleven-year-old boy, the son of a chief in what is now Nigeria. Like most village youngsters, he spent his days helping in the fields and gardens and playing with his friends, and he also learned to throw the javelin. African children like Olaudah lived surrounded by large families consisting of their parents, siblings, grandparents, aunts, uncles, and cousins. Their early life was usually sheltered, with many people taking care of them. The children had a deep respect for the elders and were expected to be polite and obedient. In the villages and the urban neighborhoods, the children were organized in groups according to their age. They remained close to their band for the rest of their life, playing, joking, and undergoing initiation (the period of instruction that led them to adulthood) together. Olaudah recalled, in his autobiography, that as the youngest of his mother's sons, he was the favorite and was always with her. But his happy existence came to a brutal end in 1756 when

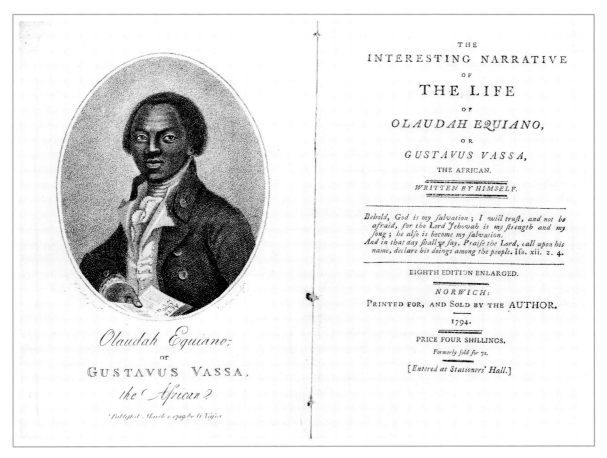

Olaudah Equiano was kidnapped as a boy from his home in Nigeria and sold and bought many times before he was able to buy his own freedom at age twenty-one. He became well known as an abolitionist and went on to publish his autobiography in 1789.

three people snatched him and his younger sister from their home while the children's parents were away.

On the coast, European and American slave dealers often tricked the people into their boats. It happened to Uncle Calina, of Sapelo Island, Georgia, who many years later told his story to his grandchildren. As he was playing on the beach near his African home with his friends as a boy, white men enticed them to the edge of the water. The children approached and were grabbed and put on board a slave ship. When the grown-ups came back from the fields, there were no children left in the village. Uncle Calina's wife, Hannah, had also been snatched away as a child. She was digging peanuts in a field with her aunt and other children when two white men seized them and put them in sacks. When they were all let out of their sacks, said Hannah, they were on a boat.[2]

Children were also tricked in a more subtle manner. John Homrn was one such victim. He was born in 1823 in Sierra Leone, where he had started school, and could read and write in English. Most African children learned a trade from their parents by observing them at work, and by being given some responsibilities with time; and John planned to become a carpenter like his father. When the boy was twelve, his father befriended an American merchant who proposed to take John so he could work as the merchant's servant for a while. After two years, during which the merchant never gave John a cent, he sold the boy as a slave in Havana, Cuba.

Being kidnapped was terrifying and unexpected. The children's entire world crumbled in an instant. The effect on the children and their families was devastating.

Prisoners of War

Other youngsters were caught in the midst of larger events that also tore their families and communities apart. Like all places, Africa had its conflicts. Some were purely local events like civil and religious wars, conflicts between rivals to the throne, and wars for economic control. But from the 1500s to the 1800s, most wars were directly provoked by the American demand for slaves. The European countries gave firearms to one ruler, for example, in exchange for his taking prisoners with the help of his powerful weapons. To protect their people, the king's neighbors needed arms, too. So they, in turn, raided other territories to get captives, whom they would exchange for guns and rifles.

During these conflicts, children were taken prisoner. It happened to Samuel Ajayi Crowther, from Nigeria. Ajayi was born about 1806 and had a good life as the great-grandson of a king. His mother was a priestess and his father, a famous weaver. Young Ajayi had learned the trade with him. He lived in Osogun, a town of 12,000. Whether in villages, small towns, or large cities, African children were in contact with people from different walks of life. There were craftspeople, soldiers, traders, musicians, singers, religious leaders, healers, and teachers. The children were stimulated by all the different activities they witnessed, the various languages they heard and learned, and the short or long trips they took with their parents to visit relatives or to move to another area. The African children were also part of the religious and social events. They prayed, they listened to the storytellers and musicians, and they danced.

Ajayi had probably taken part in all these activities during his first fifteen years, but in 1821, his life changed dramatically. His hometown was surrounded by an enemy army, and while three thousand men tried to defend their community, the women, with infants tied to their backs, children grasping their skirts, and loads on their heads, fled through the bush. Ajayi ran away with his mother, two sisters (one was only ten months old), and a cousin. The boy carried a bow and five arrows in a quiver to defend himself and his family, but, he acknowledged, "The bow I had lost in the shrub, while I was extricating myself, before I could think of making any use of it against my enemies."[3] Ajayi, his relatives, and other women and children were captured. After he was separated from his mother, the boy was sold several times. He ended up in the

Prior to their departure for the Americas, children taken by slave dealers often lived for months in damp and uncomfortable cells like this one.

harbor of Lagos, one of Nigeria's main cities, where he was bought by Portuguese slave dealers.

Pawns Become Slaves

Another group of children owed their enslavement to very different circumstances. They had been pawns. Whereas, at the time, a European went to prison for an unpaid debt, an African could give up himself or a member of his family as a pawn. The pawn worked for the creditor until the debt was cleared, but he or she still remained a free person. During the slave trade, however, the Europeans and Americans to whom a debt was owed often shipped the pawns away into slavery and sometimes seized whole families and communities, even when they had nothing to do with the original debt.

One pawn who lived a terrible experience was Kagne, a ten-year-old girl from Sierra Leone. When her father was unable to clear his debt, Kagne was put on board a Portuguese slave ship. One-third of the captives, mostly women and children, died during the voyage to America. After two months at sea Kagne disembarked in Cuba, but her frightful adventure did not end there, as you will read later.

Starvation or Slavery

In times of famine, some people had few options: They could starve to death or give themselves up for food. Parents usually started by pawning themselves and their children in exchange for something to eat. Others gave away their freedom on condition that supplies would be delivered to their young ones. Some exchanged one or two of their children for food. The agreement was that the slave dealers would feed the captive children, while the provisions received in exchange for their freedom would sustain the rest of their brothers and sisters who had remained free.

Some famines had natural causes, such as drought, flood, or parasites. But others were due to the Atlantic slave trade. The devastation produced by wars and pillages, which in turn were provoked by the trade, was a chief cause of starvation. Crops of corn, rice, millet, and vegetables were destroyed. Herds of sheep, cows, and goats starved to death. Farmers were killed or sold away, and survivors fled to remote, inhospitable areas where agriculture was impractical. Meanwhile, slave dealers bought the available food at high prices to feed their captives in the depots and while on the slave ships to the Americas, a terrible voyage called the Middle Passage. That left the poor unable to afford costly food. They fell into debt and saw their children or themselves become pawns and, in the end, slaves. With so many captives in the depots, the daily rations became small, and people who had gambled their freedom and that of their children in the hope of surviving, starved to death. In 1753, 164 men, women, and children died of hunger in the slave cells of Saint-Louis, Senegal.

The Middle Passage

However they were captured, the children had lost their family, their friends, and their independence. They were surrounded by adults and other youngsters in a state of shock and despair. Everyone was undergoing an immense personal tragedy. But with no time to mourn or even to comprehend the new situation, the captives were sent on a deadly journey. They had to walk to the sea. Some went straight to where the slave ships waited, sometimes from as far as a thousand miles away, marching for weeks. Others walked for days before being put on ships, canoes, or rafts that took them on the rivers to the Atlantic Ocean. In the slave depots, the children lived in damp, crowded cells. They had little to eat and drink and sometimes remained locked up for three or four months. Prior to departure, they underwent a barbaric ritual:

> The slaves were all put into a pen, and placed with our backs to the fire, and ordered not to look about us, and to insure obedience, a man was placed in front with a whip in his hand ready to strike the first who should dare to disobey orders; another man then went round with a hot iron, and branded us the same as they would the heads of barrels or any other inanimate goods or merchandise.[4]

All ships transported infants, who would be sold with their mothers and would become productive workers within a few years. Babies who appeared too weak to survive the journey, however, were thrown into the waters.

Conditions on the slave ships were appalling. Seasickness, open sores caused by skin rubbing on rough planks, tight shackles, infections of all kinds, filthiness, and confined space added insufferable physical pain to mental anguish.

The youngsters were often assigned to the steerage, a small area near the rudder at the rear of the vessel, considered the most uncomfortable part of the ship because of its small size and unbearable heat. The boys were generally allowed an individual space of about five feet by fourteen inches (1.5 meters by 36 centimeters) and girls, four feet by twelve inches (1.2 meters by 30 centimeters). The height between the floor and the platform above the captives' heads was from eighteen to twenty-four inches (46 to 61 centimeters). Accidents were common. The youngest children sometimes had to be pulled from the tubs the captives used to relieve themselves.

The children were considered harmless, unlike the men, who often organized revolts when they were unshackled on deck. Thus, children could stay on deck for longer periods than the adults, with the result that in bad weather some were swept away by high waves or drowned when the ship pitched violently. In addition, female captives, including young girls, had to face sickening worries of their own. They were often the victims of sexual abuse by the crew, which might number from thirty to seventy men. In addition to rape, some girls had to bear unwanted pregnancies and suffer sexually transmitted diseases that left some of them unable to have children.

There was little to eat on the slave ships, and the captives received only one pint of water a day. Those too sick to eat were severely punished. "I have seen some of these poor African prisoners . . . hourly whipped for not eating. This

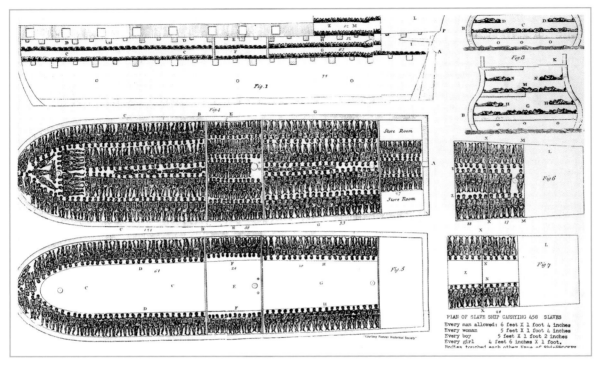

Along with the adults, children were usually transported to the Americas in vessels like this British slave ship, Brookes. The horrible conditions were made worse by disease and starvation, and travel sometimes lasted three months.

indeed was often the case with myself," recalled Olaudah Equiano, who was eleven at the time.[5]

To be confined in a small space with up to seven hundred people certainly gave rise to tensions and irritation. But Africans and European witnesses alike stressed the solidarity and sense of kinship that bonded the men, women, and children who went through the Middle Passage together. For the youngest children, these qualities were essential. If older children and grown-ups had not helped them get food and drink, go to the tubs, climb up to the deck; and if they had not protected the children during the numerous revolts that erupted on the ships, and made efforts to alleviate the youngsters' fears and depression, these children simply could not have survived.

But goodwill and kindness could not save everyone, and hundreds of thousands of children died on their way to the Americas. They died of scurvy, which made them bleed. They suffered acute dysentery, which gave them terrible abdominal pains and bloody diarrhea. They endured extreme dehydration caused by various diseases and by intense perspiration in the lower decks, where the temperature often reached more than 110 degrees F (43 degrees C). Smallpox was a fierce killer of captives, who died covered with blood let loose by their shedding scabs. Others were simply thrown overboard when food and water became too scarce or an epidemic broke out. The shortest trips between the coast of Africa and the Americas lasted six weeks, the longest more than three months. About 20 percent of the Africans who were forced onto the slave ships died during the Middle Passage.

From Freedom to Bondage

The children who survived had a dreadful future to contemplate. They disembarked in America with weak and stiff limbs, infections, and diseases of all sorts. One youngster recalled: "When we arrived at Charleston [South Carolina], I was not able to stand. It was more than a week after I left the ship before I could straighten my limbs."[6]

As they thought about what they had already endured since they were torn away from their families, the children could only imagine and fear what the rest of their existence would be. Despite these terrible circumstances, the young Africans went on. Some were extraordinary children who overcame appalling conditions.

At first enslaved by a Virginia planter, Olaudah Equiano—the young Nigerian boy abducted with his sister—

was sold and lived in Great Britain for six years before being sold again. This time, he became the property of an American ship owner who traded in the Caribbean islands. Olaudah became a clerk and was an assistant to the ship's captain, until he was able to buy his own freedom at age twenty-one. He then made his living as a sailor and traveled the Mediterranean Sea, the Arctic Ocean, and Central America. An active and well-known abolitionist, Equiano published his autobiography in 1789. It was a best-seller and went through thirty-six editions in English, German, and Dutch.

On June 28, 1839, Kagne, the ten-year-old pawn from Sierra Leone, and fifty-two others—three of them children like her—were put on board the Cuban schooner *La Amistad*. On the third night, led by twenty-five-year-old Singbe (also called Cinque), the Africans took control of the ship and ordered the crew to bring them back to West Africa. For two months the ship wandered the seas, steered at night toward the American continent by the crew. Some of the Africans died of hunger and thirst. The boat finally landed on Long Island, New York, and the Africans were jailed for rebellion and murder. After a long trial the thirty-five survivors sailed back to Sierra Leone. Kagne, who like several others in the group had learned to read and write, arrived in Freetown in January 1842, after one of the most frightful adventures a child could endure.

Salih Bilali, abducted as he was horseback riding, became the head driver or foreman of the slaves of a large plantation on St. Simons Island, Georgia. A practicing Muslim all his life, he managed to get a Qur'an (the Muslim holy book) in Arabic on a remote Georgia island. Salih Bilali had been a free boy for fourteen years and a slave for more than sixty; but he had succeeded in maintaining his literacy in Arabic and in becoming a manager.

Samuel Ajayi Crowther, the young prisoner of war, started his dreadful journey to Brazil but never got there. It was 1822, and most countries had abolished the international slave trade.[7] The British Navy seized the slave ships it could find (the majority went undetected) and unloaded their human cargo all over America. Nevertheless, about 80,000 men, women, and children, including Ajayi, were rescued between 1819 and 1871. The boy was sent to Sierra Leone. Within six months he had learned to read and write, and he later became a well-known Anglican bishop.

John Homrn, who had been tricked into bondage by his father's friend at the age of twelve, was enslaved in Cuba and Puerto Rico. There, he managed to send letters to his family in Sierra Leone to obtain evidence of his free status. When nothing worked, he hid in a boat bound for England and crossed the Atlantic as a stowaway. In 1847, at the age of twenty-four, he finally returned home.

Olaudah Equiano, Kagne, Samuel Ajayi Crowther, Salih Bilali, John Homrn, and many others were brilliant children. They shaped their own lives as much as they could and realized great feats against tremendous odds. Although most African children remained anonymous, they too in many ways were little heroes. They had started life as carefree and protected as other children but had to quickly master physical and psychological survival skills. The African boys and girls had to come to terms with their new inferior status without letting it destroy their minds and their hearts. They learned new languages, nurtured families, built communities, developed their talents, and transmitted to the next generation what they had retained of their native cultures. The African children demonstrated a profound sense of self-esteem, considerable resiliency, and courage well beyond their years.

Chapter Two

Enslaved from Birth

After they disembarked from ships in America, the Africans were sold on slave markets, and then sent to plantations, some of which were located far away from the coast. There the African children met boys and girls who looked like them. However, if they had been able to communicate through a common language, they would have discovered immediately that, although they were now going to share the same hard life, they came from very different worlds. The children the young Africans met were born in America and were the children or grandchildren of Africans who had been shipped years before. These children had never been free. Unlike the African youths, they had grown up knowing they were the property of someone else, just like a horse or a plow, and that they could be sold away from their families and friends. They were aware that they could not go anywhere without a pass, which was written permission from their owner stating where they were allowed to go and for how long. The children born in bondage knew they had no rights and no good future, and that they were at the bottom of society. Thomas Jones, from North Carolina, described these feelings:

> My recollections of early life are associated with poverty, suffering and shame. I was made to feel, in my boyhood's first experience, that I was inferior and degraded, and that I must pass through life in a dependent and suffering condition.[1]

It was a depressing realization for young people, who had a whole lifetime of privation and humiliation to contemplate. Fortunately, they could count on their parents for love and consolation, something most of the African-born children could no longer do.

Children and Families

The strong bond that existed between parents and children was stressed repeatedly by people who had been slaves. They noted that families were all the more precious because they represented the only joy, warmth, and source of pride that parents and children could find. Even after long hours in the fields, parents still made time to tell stories, and to teach their sons and daughters to cook, sew, make baskets and pots, and fish and hunt. They worked hard to shield their children from the horrors of slavery and to provide them with some comfort and pleasure.

But, as loving as the parents might be, they were not able to offer any protection against the overseers (the white men who kept watch over and directed and controlled the work of the slaves) and the slave owners. Because the enslaved children generally played with the white boys and girls of the plantations until they were eight or ten years old, they were able to catch a glimpse of the other children's lives. They saw their companions run to their parents for safety, for example, while they could not. Jacob Stroyer's experience was typical. As a young boy tending horses, he was whipped by a white groom. When he ran crying to his father (who had been abducted from Sierra Leone as a boy) expecting him to scold the groom, he was bitterly disappointed. His father sent him back, saying he could not do anything for him. Jacob then asked his mother to intervene. When she did, the groom flogged both her and Jacob. The whippings continued and the boy decided to fight back, but his father explained:

> You must not do that, because if you do he will say that your mother and I advised you to do it, and it will make it hard for your mother and me, as well as for yourself . . . I can do nothing more than to pray to the Lord to hasten the time when these things shall be done away; that is all I can do.[2]

The children were sons and daughters and, as such, they were expected to obey their parents. However, they were the property of someone else who had absolute control over them. This situation caused tensions and conflicts for the children. Harriet Jacobs described an incident in which both her father and her owner had called her brother Willie at the same time:

> [Willie] finally concluded to go to his mistress. When my father reproved him for it, he said, "You both called me, and I didn't know which I ought to go to first." "You are *my* child," replied our father, "and when I call you, you should come immediately, if you have to pass through fire and water."[3]

Willie's father was a proud man whose scolding was meant to teach his son that although a slave, he was still a father who had to be respected and obeyed. Caught between parents who had no rights and owners who could sell them away from their families, children had to make choices that sometimes resulted in punishment from both sides.

Slavery had another horrifying effect on black families. As much as parents loved their children, they were sometimes relieved when the youngsters died, and some mothers actually killed their children in order to spare them a lifetime of suffering. Lewis Clarke, who fled slavery in Kentucky for freedom in Canada, explained:

> There was a slave mother near where I lived, who took her child into the cellar and killed it. She did it to prevent being separated from her child. . . . At the death of many a slave child, I have seen the two feelings struggling in the bosom of a mother—joy, that it was beyond the reach of the slave monsters, and the natural grief of a mother over her child. In the presence of the master, grief seems to predominate; when away from them, they rejoice that there is one whom the slave-killer will never torment.[4]

Many women, like the former slave Bethany Veney, had a particular reason to wish their newborn daughters could die. Veney mentioned that she knew, from experience, that her daughter would probably be sexually molested by slave owners, and that no law would protect her. "I felt all this," she wrote, "and would have been glad if we could have died together there and then."[5]

The Mulatto Children

Among the slave children born in America, one group of youngsters lived in a unique situation: Their mothers were black slave women and their fathers were free white men. During slavery, owners and overseers often forced themselves upon women and girls over whom they had absolute control.

Girls grew up with the constant fear of being raped. Children of both sexes dreaded seeing their mothers and sisters molested while their fathers could do nothing to protect them. These practices resulted in the creation of a large group of mixed-race children called mulattoes. The census of 1860 revealed that out of 4.4 million black persons living in the United States, 600,000 were officially of mixed race. The real numbers were probably much higher because the slave population and the free blacks were never counted adequately. Moreover, it was the census taker who decided, based upon the color of the respondent, who was a mulatto and who was not. The overwhelming majority of mixed-race people were slaves, and, according to most accounts, their lives were especially miserable. Many youngsters knew who their fathers were, but they were completely ignored by these men, most of whom were already married to white women. To father children outside of marriage was considered a sin, and the law prohibited sexual relations between the races. Thus, the presence of mixed-race children was a constant reminder to the fathers that according to religion, the law, and morality, they were guilty.

Some men regarded their relationships with their female slaves as legitimate unions and recognized their mixed-race children. They sometimes sent the children north or to Europe, where they became free. Although leaving for the unknown was difficult and frightening, it was the best opportunity available to the children. Other responsible and caring fathers kept their children in the South, but had them learn a trade, gave them their freedom, and sometimes left them money and land when they died. Yet these were exceptions, and most mixed-race children grew up as poor slaves witnessing daily the far easier life of their white half brothers and sisters.

According to most testimonies, the people who made the mulatto children's lives especially unbearable were their fathers' white wives. The half-white children were proof of the husbands' infidelity. Because it was not acceptable, in those times, for women to openly criticize their spouses, these women generally turned their anger toward the mulatto children and the children's mothers. Moses Roper, of North Carolina, was told that his father's wife had tried to kill him with a large stick and a club when he was born. The murder of mulatto babies by white women was rare, but several slaves mentioned that they were beaten, whipped, and mistreated by their fathers' wives. As Lewis Clarke stated:

> There are no slaves that are so badly abused as those that are related to some of the [white] women, or the children of their own husband; it seems as though they never could hate these quite bad enough.[6]

The percentage of mulattoes who ran away was higher than their percentage in the enslaved population; this suggests that they lived in especially difficult circumstances. The advertisements for their capture often mentioned whip marks on their backs and even on their faces.

Besides problems with the white wives, conflicts could also arise with the fathers' white children. Some fathers gave clothes or food to their mulatto children and treated them better than the other slaves. This created resentment among the slave owners' white children who disliked the attention given by their fathers to their half brothers and sisters. When problems became too difficult to handle, the solution was frequently the same: The mulatto children were sold away. Many fathers did not mind selling their own children at a profit. But Frederick Douglass, a mulatto who fled slavery and became a prominent abolitionist, stated that some men sold their children to protect them. Young mulattoes would be safer far from the wives and children of their fathers.

The fate of mixed-race girls, in particular, could be tragic. The beautiful mulatto, quadroon (a mulatto mother and white father), and octoroon (a quadroon mother and white father) youngsters often became "fancy girls." Their skin color ranged from very light brown to white, and they were sold at high prices to become prostitutes or mistresses. "These white children of slavery," wrote a Swedish woman who traveled in the South, "become, for the most part, victims of crime, and sink into the deepest degradation."[7] Some slave dealers specialized in the sale of light-skinned girls aged twelve and up. In some instances, the traders were the fathers of these children. As recounted by Moses Roper:

> The traders will often sleep with the best-looking female slaves . . . and they will often have many children in the year . . . Through this villainy [they] will make an immense profit of this intercourse, by selling the babe with its mother.[8]

Sales and Separation

During slavery, the children and their parents lived in constant fear of being separated. The first of January was the most dreaded date of the year because on that day, traditionally, people were sold or hired out to other plantations.

The men, women, and children who were going to be sold were never told in advance. The slaveholders believed that they had the right to dispose of their property any time and in any manner they wished. The people who had just been sold had to leave immediately, without as much as a good-bye to their parents or children. Katie Rowe, of Arkansas, described a terrible but ordinary scene she saw during slavery: Some

HEWLETT & BRIGHT.

SALE OF

VALUABLE

SLAVES,

(On account of departure)

The Owner of the following named and valuable Slaves, being on the eve of departure for Europe, will cause the same to be offered for sale, at the NEW EXCHANGE, corner of St. Louis and Chartres streets, on *Saturday,* May 16, at Twelve o'Clock, *viz.*

1. **SARAH,** a mulatress, aged 45 years, a good cook and accustomed to house work in general, is an excellent and faithful nurse for sick persons, and in every respect a first rate character.

2. **DENNIS,** her son, a mulatto, aged 24 years, a first rate cook and steward for a vessel, having been in that capacity for many years on board one of the Mobile packets; is strictly honest, temperate, and a first rate subject.

3. **CHOLE,** a mulatress, aged 36 years, she is, without execption, one of the most competent servants in the country, a first rate washer and ironer, does up lace, a good cook, and for a bachelor who wishes a house-keeper she would be invaluable; she is also a good ladies' maid, having travelled to the North in that capacity.

4. **FANNY,** her daughter, a mulatress, aged 16 years, speaks French and English, is a superior hair-dresser, (pupil of Guilliac,) a good seamstress and ladies' maid, is smart, intelligent, and a first rate character.

5. **DANDRIDGE,** a mulatoo, aged 26 years, a first rate dining-room servant, a good painter and rough carpenter, and has but few equals for honesty and sobriety.

6. **NANCY,** his wife, aged about 24 years, a confidential house servant, good seamstress, mantuamaker and tailoress, a good cook, washer and ironer, etc.

7. **MARY ANN,** her child, a creole, aged 7 years, speaks French and English, is smart, active and intelligent.

8. **FANNY or FRANCES,** a mulatress, aged 22 years, is a first rate washer and ironer, good cook and house servant, and has an excellent character.

9. **EMMA,** an orphan, aged 10 or 11 years, speaks French and English, has been in the country 7 years, has been accustomed to waiting on table, sewing etc.; is intelligent and active.

10. **FRANK,** a mulatto, aged about 32 years speaks French and English, is a first rate hostler and coachman, understands perfectly well the management of horses, and is, in every respect, a first rate character, with the exception that he will occasionally drink, though not an habitual drunkard.

☞ All the above named Slaves are acclimated and excellent subjects; they were purchased by their present vendor many years ago, and will, therefore, be severally warranted against all vices and maladies prescribed by law, save and except FRANK, who is fully guaranteed in every other respect but the one above mentioned.

TERMS:—One-half Cash, and the other half in notes at Six months, drawn and endorsed to the satisfaction of the Vendor, with special mortgage on the Slaves until final payment.   The Acts of Sale to be passed before WILLIAM BOSWELL, *Notary Public,* at the expense of the Purchaser.

New-Orleans, May 13, 1835.

PRINTED BY BENJAMIN LEVY.

Before a slave auction, flyers like this one were posted in town squares. These posters advertised the good qualities and physical characteristics of the people who would be on the auction block.

young children were playing, when their owner and another man to whom he owed money came by. The master told him to chose a child as payment for the debt. The man took one and rode away. Another young girl, Elizabeth Keckley, witnessed a most degrading sale. Her owner did not have enough money to buy all the hogs he wanted, so to make up the difference, he took the cook's young son and "placed [him] in the scales, and [he] was sold, like the hogs, at so much per pound."[9]

Those were horrific episodes for the children who were, in an instant, snatched from their families and communities to face a completely unknown future, sometimes hundreds of miles from their home. When cotton cultivation spread to Alabama, Mississippi, and Georgia, about one million men, women, and children were displaced from the Atlantic Coast to the Lower South. Later, in the 1840s, Alabama exported thousands of enslaved people to the new territories of Texas and Arkansas.

On occasions when the parents happened to be present, they would plead with the owner and the dealer to let their children go. Moses Grandy, of North Carolina, described what happened to his mother when one of her young sons was sold:

> My mother, frantic with grief, resisted their taking her child away: She was beaten and held down: She fainted; and when she came to herself, her boy was gone. She made much outcry, for which the master tied her up to a peach tree in the yard and flogged her.[10]

Occasionally, free boys and girls were kidnapped and sold as slaves. The passage, in 1850, of the Fugitive Slave Act authorized slaveholders to take possession of runaway slaves anywhere in the United States without trial, and required

Once in America, men, women, and children were auctioned off and handed over to the highest bidder; sometimes sold and resold many times throughout their lives.

citizens to aid in their capture. One effect of this law was that countless free people were kidnapped, because when slave catchers did not find the runaways they were chasing, they seized anyone they could. Whole families from the North were abducted at night and transported to the South where they were sold in different states. Some of the slave catchers were not looking for fugitives at all, but just for people they could sell. J. W. Lindsay recalled:

In this painting, newly purchased slaves are being transported to work for their new owners. Bought by different people, mothers and children, husbands and wives, and other family members were often separated and sent to distant parts of the country during this heartbreaking process.

I was born free, but was kidnapped, when a child, like thousands of others. I was taken from Washington city and carried to West Tennessee. My parents advertised me in the papers, and the individuals who kidnapped me carried me to South Carolina, Georgia and Alabama.[11]

Lindsay remained enslaved until he was a grown man.

Another dreadful experience for children was to see their parents or siblings taken away. John Walker, who was sold five times before he ran away, endured such an agonizing episode:

> When I was 7 years old, they sold my father. He wouldn't let them whip him, so several men overpowered him and put him on a horse and took him away. I sat on the fence a-cryin.[12]

People were purchased directly on the plantations or were taken to town to be sold at auction, a distressing and humiliating process. Men, women, and children, sometimes entire families, were put on a platform. The auctioneer stated their age and skills, and half stripped, the people had to exhibit their good health and ability to work hard by showing their teeth and their muscles. The buyers then bid on them.

Traders, called speculators, whose job was to buy and sell slaves, would purchase several and gather them in a "coffle." A coffle was a large group of people who were made to walk from plantation to plantation, from state to state, so that they could be sold along the way. The adults and the older boys were generally chained together. The younger children were put on a wagon drawn by horse or mule.

According to the estimates of historians, more than half the men, women, and children held in servitude in the United States were sold several times during their lives, each time leaving families and loved ones behind.

Chapter Three

Life and Work

Poor living conditions and grueling work were the daily reality of the children growing up in slavery. They experienced extreme poverty with its health problems, feelings of insecurity, and unfulfilled needs. Childhood was short, for they were compelled to start working at an early age.

Most enslaved men, women, and children lived in the countryside; about 10 percent were in the cities, where they worked as artisans and domestics. Plantations of cotton, indigo, rice, sugarcane, and tobacco required numerous workers and were located in the South, which held the vast majority of the slave community. Some plantations were very large and could utilize several hundred workers, but most counted fewer than twenty. But wherever they lived and worked, the children shared a number of characteristics.

They were shorter, on average, than their West Indian counterparts and much shorter than the children who live today in Africa, Asia, or Latin America. This peculiarity was due to the poor health of expectant mothers. The women's diet was inadequate, and they did backbreaking work. Consequently, their babies were generally born small.

Disease and death often marked the first years of a child's life. Children suffered from intestinal worms, tetanus, fevers, measles, pneumonia, inflammation of the lungs, and whooping cough. When sick, they were treated not by doctors but by elder slave nurses. Most of the nurses' knowledge had originated in Africa and had been passed on from one generation to the next. The nurses used whatever medications were accessible to them, such as herbs, bark, and roots. Some of their folk remedies worked very well, but others did not. Slave children were four times more likely to die of tetanus, for example, than were white children.

The number of deaths on any given plantation was staggering. Fanny Anne Kemble, the wife of a Georgia slaveholder who owned five hundred people, conducted a survey of the infant mortality, or death rate, on her plantation. She asked the women how many children they had given birth to, and how many were still living. Nancy had lost two children out of three. Leah had had six children, three of whom were dead. Five of Sukey's eleven children had died, and Sarah had lost five of her seven children. The nine women Fanny Kemble interviewed had had a total of twelve miscarriages and fifty-five children, twenty-nine of whom had not survived. Even though this seems like a terrible record, Kemble stressed that "people on this plantation are well-off, and consider themselves well-off, in comparison with the slaves on some of the neighboring estates."[1]

Because supervision was inadequate, children were prone to accidents. They burned themselves by getting too close to a fire or fell from steps. As they went barefoot, they walked on nails, glass, or other sharp objects that cut their feet, resulting in infections. The lack of shoes during the winter months resulted in painful frostbite.

On small plantations where there was nobody else to care for their babies, mothers strapped them to their backs and took them to the fields, where they laid the babies in the shade on a piece of fabric or a pallet. Some made hammocks that they secured between two trees. The women stopped working just long enough to nurse the infants three or four times a day under the vigilant eye of the overseer, who hurried them back to work with a crack of his whip. The babies spent the day alone at the mercy of flies, mosquitoes, ants, bees, and snakes. Accidents were common. Some infants crawled away and fell into ditches; others fell from the hammocks.

On larger estates, young children were left at the nursery. It was nothing more than an empty room with a dirt floor where babies slept and infants crawled under the care of an elderly woman and several young boys and girls. The babies were given bottles, or the young nurses took them to the fields to be breast fed by their mothers. On some plantations, women had two breaks a day to feed their children at the nursery before going back to the fields. But on other planta-tions, mothers were not allowed even to see their babies during the week. Nurses breast fed all the babies of the estate and gave them back to their mothers on Saturday.

As they grew up, the children discovered the world of slavery, and the realities of plantation life: hunger, poverty, work, and punishment.

Food

Slave narratives mention over and over how hungry the chil-dren were. On the average plantation, the children's food allowance was one pint of dry grits, rice, or cornmeal per week. Meat was scarce and, when given, was allowed in very small quantities. One planter, for example, who was consid-ered generous, allotted 30 pounds (13.7 kilograms) of meat a week to feed 130 children. Most children and adults had their only taste of meat when the boys and men had a successful hunt. They used dogs and traps because they were not allowed

The food given to children was barely adequate; meals usually consisted of simple grits or mush, rarely including any meat. This scene shows a group of children being fed, perhaps in a nursery setting.

to carry guns, and they had to hunt at night, by the light of pitch-pine torches, because they worked all day. The hunters brought their families opossums, raccoons, rabbits, wild turkeys, partridges, and squirrels.

To complement their diet, the children spent a great deal of time in their parents' gardens. The slaveholders encouraged their laborers to grow their own food because it made the people healthier and reduced the planters' costs. Gardening was done at night, after work, by the light of the moon and of lights made by burning grease in a frying pan. Men, women, and children, working side by side, grew peas, squash, sweet potatoes, cabbage, greens, corn, and turnips. Some added tobacco and cotton that they sold to buy fabric, shoes, hats, and other items not provided by the slave owners. When their work was done, the children roamed the woods in search of walnuts and wild berries.

On most plantations, the children's meals were served in a trough. Crumbled bread, peas, sauce, or buttermilk were poured into the tub and the youngsters ate with their hands or with seashells. Annie Burton never forgot how and what she and her companions ate:

> We children had no supper, and only a little piece of bread or something of the kind in the morning. Our dishes consisted of one wooden bowl, and oyster shells were our spoons. This bowl served for about fifteen children, and often the dogs and the ducks and the peafowl had a dip in it. Sometimes we had buttermilk and bread in our bowl, sometimes greens or bones.[2]

A common dish for the children was what they called "mush": corn flour in hot water served with molasses. They generally disliked it, hoping some day to taste one of the favorites, hopping John, a mixture of cow peas, rice, and bacon.

Dress

Boys and girls were dressed the same. They all wore a long shirt with a hole for the head and two for the arms. The boys' garment was called a "shirttail" and the girls wore a "shift." Adults and children usually received one change of clothes in winter and another one in summer. As a rule, the youngsters did not get underwear. The shirttails and shifts were of poor quality, and the author and activist Booker T. Washington recalled that the rough fabrics felt like "a dozen or more chestnut burrs" rubbing on his skin. Wearing these clothes, he said, was the "most trying ordeal" he was forced to endure.[3]

The shirts were uncomfortable for another reason: They were handed out without regard for the actual size of the child or the rate of his or her growth. Since the same garment had to be worn every day for months, slave children endured ragged, dirty clothes, disgusting to see and wear. When the garments were completely torn, the children remained naked until the next distribution. This was a common sight on Southern plantations, and travelers from other parts of the country were often shocked at seeing naked or half-naked boys and girls, sometimes as old as fourteen years of age. When slavery had ended, many men and women recalled the utter shame they felt as children at being forced to stay naked by contemptuous and greedy slave owners.

Shoes were unknown to the children until they became teenagers. The Reverend G. C. Brown of South Carolina said that, like many others, his father

> wrapped his feet in gunny sacks. He said you could track him through his blood in the snow as he went out to bring the cows home during those snowy nights. In the morning he'd get up and run the cow up from where he slept all night to warm his feet.[4]

Housing

"We lived in little log houses daubed with mud and didn't have no beds—slept on the ground on pallets."[5] When Rose Holman, of Mississippi, described the house she grew up in, she could have been describing almost all the lodging quarters of the slaves. Those cabins were usually one room ten or twelve feet square. They had a dirt floor, one door, and one fireplace. Many did not have a window. People stuffed cotton, mud, and rags in the spaces between the logs, but this did little to prevent the wind, rain, and cold from affecting the residents.

A single cabin usually housed a whole family. There could be as many as a dozen people living in one shack. Parents and children ate, rested, slept, and dressed in the same room. In many areas, however, the overcrowding and lack of privacy were even worse, as described by Jacob Stroyer:

> Most of the cabins . . . were built so as to contain two families. . . . When there were no partitions, each family would fit up its own part as it could; sometimes they got old boards and nailed them up, stuffing the cracks with old rags; when they could not get boards, they hung up old clothes.[6]

To save money and because of a lack of consideration for the people, slave quarters were not provided with outhouses. The people therefore had to go to the bushes to relieve themselves, and it was sometimes hard, as noted by former slaves, to find a place to hide.

The interior of the cabins was normally bare because slaveholders did not provide furniture, and men and women had to build whatever they needed if they could find the necessary tools and planks. Some men were good carpenters and built tables, chairs, and beds, while women made mattresses and filled them with hay, moss, or corn shucks. To keep their families comfortable at night, they sewed heavy quilts and stuffed them with cotton or moss. More commonly, parents and children alike slept on pallets or on the floor with

These slave quarters in Florida are typical of the conditions under which people lived. Dirt floors, overcrowding, and inadequate protection from the weather made living in these homes uncomfortable and unpleasant.

blankets issued every two or three years. Josiah Henson, who grew up in Maryland, described his sleeping arrangements:

> Our beds were collections of straw and old rags, thrown down in the corner and boxed in with boards; a single blanket the only covering. Our favorite way of sleeping, however, was on a plank, our heads raised on an old jacket and our feet toasting before the smoldering fire.[7]

Although the cabins were uncomfortable, they provided children with the only safe environment they knew. Surrounded by siblings, parents, and grandparents, they became children again, and they could relax and forget the hardships of the day.

But around four every morning, they had to get up and prepare for their day as young slaves. Men, women, and children, still tired from the hard labor of the day before, walked to their place of work: the fields, the yards, or the master's house.

Young Children's Chores

For many children, work started as soon as they reached five or six years of age. In the slaveholders' houses, chores for the youngest children were abundant. They gathered and brought armloads of wood for the fireplaces and the kitchen. They continuously fanned the owners and their guests with turkey feathers to keep the heat, the flies, and the mosquitoes away. They washed their masters' feet and scratched their heads until they fell asleep. The children polished the brass doorknobs and scrubbed the floors. They ran errands and helped the laundresses, the weavers, the quilt makers, and the cook. They brought buckets of water on their heads from the spring or well to the house.

Even though these young workers were around the house all day and served their owners fine food, they were often as hungry as the field hands. Jake Maddox, of Georgia, recalled that the children would get the chicken feet out of the garbage, roast them, and gnaw the bones. "I recollect seeing one biscuit crust, one morning," stated Alex McCinney. "They threw it out to the dogs, and I beat the dog to it."[8]

In the yards, there were many tasks to perform. The children fed the goats, hogs, horses, sheep, and chickens. They

In these two photographs, children are among the laborers picking cotton in Georgia (left) and transporting it in South Carolina (below). Children often helped the adults during picking time, sometimes acting as scarecrows to frighten away the birds.

milked the cows. They swept the yards and pulled up weeds. They brought buckets of water to the field hands and shucked the corn.

On tobacco plantations, young children checked the tobacco leaves, took off any worms, and killed them. The usual punishment for not doing a thorough job was several lashes or a bite of the worms. For one six year old, Nancy Williams, of Virginia, it was even worse: Her master grabbed a handful of worms and stuffed them into her mouth.

Work on the hot and humid sugar plantations of Louisiana was tiring. The children loaded carts with the sugarcane that the older children and adults had cut. They drove the carts to the mill. Then they unloaded them and placed the stalks on rollers that carried them to the place where they were ground.

On Georgia and South Carolina rice plantations, the children worked in ditches in the rice paddies. At harvest, they pounded the rice in a mortar to remove the husks.

The cotton planters used young children to help the adults during picking time. Before the invention of the cotton gin in 1793, children patiently removed the seeds, burrs, and sticks from the cotton flowers. In the nineteenth century, they ginned the cotton by turning the crank and filling sacks; and they helped the women card and spin the thread.

Young children also worked as scarecrows. They went to the fields early in the morning and stayed until dark, gesturing and making noise all day long to scare away the birds. On Texas ranches, they helped tend the horses and cattle and were called "cow boys."

A common occupation for girls was caring for the smaller children of the plantation, both black and white. They carried the children around, played with them, and made sure they did not fall down or get close to the fire. Some nurses were extremely young. Elizabeth Keckley—who later became the seamstress of President Lincoln's wife—was in charge of her owners' baby when she was only four years old. Ellen Betts, of Louisiana, remembered that some white babies were so fat and she so small that she used to carry their feet while another girl carried their head.

Older Children's Work

Becoming a full-time worker, at around age twelve, was as much dreaded as it was anticipated with some pleasure. On the bad side, it was the beginning of backbreaking work. On the good side, this new step meant getting the same amount of food as the adults. And, not to be taken lightly, the satisfaction of receiving, at last, underwear, pants, skirts, and sometimes shoes.

The workday started around 4:30 in the morning because the slaves had to be in the fields, which were sometimes distant from their living quarters, by daybreak. Work ended when it was too dark to see, but at harvesttime, men, women, and children were often required to work up to fifteen hours. Most children became field hands. They plowed, hoed, picked tobacco leaves, and cut the sugarcane and the hay. On most cotton plantations, children were required to pick 150 pounds (68 kilograms) of cotton a day. They planted and harvested rice, indigo, corn, and vegetables. They cleared the land and the marshes, felled trees, split rails, and helped build fences, levees, and houses.

In the owner's house, whether on the plantations or in the cities, young domestics were on call twenty-four hours a day, every day. They sewed, washed, and ironed the clothes. They helped prepare and cook the food, waited on tables, and washed the dishes. They dusted, polished, and swept. They cleaned the windows and the floors and helped the owners and their children wash, dress, and undress.

Young girls were often put in charge of caring for the younger children on the plantation, sometimes working as nannies to their owners' children. The original caption for this photo reads, "H. E. Hayward (infant) with slave nurse Louisa."

Some youngsters were placed as apprentices. The boys learned carpentry, masonry, plastering, and bricklaying. Some made harnesses and shoes and tanned leather. Others became skillful blacksmiths. The girls learned their trade with seamstresses, cooks, embroiderers, quilt makers, weavers, and laundresses. The apprentices who were lucky enough to become free could make a decent living and pass on their useful skills to their children.

Punishments

To a slaveholder, the only value of the slaves was the quantity of work they could produce and the number of children they could have, because these children in turn would become workers without wages. To make sure that the people would work as hard as possible, not run away from the plantations, and accept their servitude without attempting to revolt, the slaveholders used cruel punishments designed to instill fear and obedience in their workers.

Growing up in slavery meant seeing and experiencing extreme brutality. The children, from their very first years, marched to the sound of the whip. Not even infants were spared. Henry Bibb, a fugitive from Kentucky who became a well-known abolitionist, recalled that his "infant child was also frequently flogged . . . for crying, until his skin was bruised literally purple."[9]

Children were punished sometimes for the slightest mistake, or because they had come late when called, had broken something, or had given a defiant look. They were slapped, kicked, and had their hair pulled out, but whipping was the most common form of punishment. It was done on the naked backs and buttocks with a cat-o'-nine-tails, a whip made of nine leather straps with knots at the ends. Another instrument of abuse was the paddle. A former slave described

Brutality toward enslaved people was not uncommon. Punishments, like this lashing, were designed to instill fear and obedience.

it as "a board six inches broad, and eight inches long, with twelve gimlet holes in it; each of these holes raised a blister every time a blow was inflicted."[10]

Whipping was extremely painful, and after several lashes, the skin was cut and blood ran to the ground. It was a habit to rub salt, pepper, or vinegar on the fresh lacerations as an added, extremely cruel punishment. To ease the pain and to prevent garments from sticking to the bloody cuts, women used to put grease on the wounds.

Even though they were young, the children could receive extreme punishments. Some beatings and kicks resulted in broken legs or arms, and there were instances of youngsters burned with hot irons. And, like the adults, some children were beaten and whipped to death.

Chapter Four

Children at Play

Until they started work, most children could play freely. Their time was theirs, and because the adults, working from early morning until night, could not be around, the children spent their days as they wished. Nevertheless, some former slaves remembered that they never played—the only thing they could recall was work. Of course, situations varied from one place to the other.

Where there were few laborers, the children were certainly used as much as possible. In the cities, they had no space and were under constant surveillance. But many youths, especially on large plantations, managed to have a good time in their early years.

Leisure, Families, and Community

The leisure activities of the children started at home. Those lucky enough to live with their parents and grandparents learned about times and places they had not experienced.

Fishing from a bridge was a simple way for these children to enjoy some of their precious and extremely limited free time.

Many men and women remembered stories their parents, grandparents, or neighbors told them about growing up as free children in Africa. There were descriptions of unknown fruits and vegetables, of wonderful crops and strange animals. And there were many tales. Storytelling was an activity much enjoyed by parents and children. African tales that portray animals such as the rabbit, hyena, and spider were told again and again to the delight of the children. Brother Rabbit, swift and smart, was the favorite character. The selfish and dumb hyena, called Bouki, was mocked and despised.[1] One reason these trickster tales, as they are known, were popular is they showed small and cunning animals who, because they were smart, outwitted the mighty kings of the forest. Enslaved children could relate to tales that showed that the weak could still win over the powerful and the strong with intelligence and slyness.

Scary tales of ghosts and spirits were plenty. Older children, in particular, delighted in relating frightening stories that scared the younger children. Parents told their children that Raw Head and Bloody Bones lived in the woods and ate children for supper. The purpose of these tales was to make sure that the youngsters would not go out at night or venture into unknown or dangerous territory. It was especially important for the children not to leave the plantation alone, because patrollers (groups of white men and older boys) roamed the countryside and arrested and whipped the slaves who could not show a pass.

On Saturday nights, some plantations held "frolics" by the light of fat kindling or torches of kindling wood. The musicians stretched a cowhide over a cheese box to make a tambourine, knocked on tin buckets and pans, and blew quills. James Bolton, of Georgia, remembered them fondly:

> Quills was a row of whistles made out of reeds or sometimes they made them out of bark. Every whistle in the row was a different tone and you could play any kind of tune you wants if you had a good row of quills.[2]

To the music of these homemade instruments, parents and children sang and danced the Turkey Trot and the Buzzard Lope. "Mary Jane" was a well-liked ring dance; when the music stopped, the dancers moved their feet quickly while they sang.

Singing and dancing were a major form of entertainment. "Frolics," as the dances were sometimes known, were great fun for everyone, young and old alike.

A favorite community event was corn-shucking. At night, large groups of men and women, some rented out from other plantations, shucked huge quantities of corn. It was a tedious activity, but the people turned it into a memorable social event. Former slaves remembered it as a good time because there was abundant food, music, singing, joking, and friendly rivalry between teams of workers. After dinner, the boys had competitions of their own, such as wrestling, racing, and jumping.

Holidays

Christmas, Independence Day, sometimes Thanksgiving, and the day marking the end of harvest were exciting days. What made them so special was the profusion of food. Parents received extra rations of pork, molasses, and flour, and the women made biscuits. Being hungry most of the year, the children looked forward to the big meals. There was usually a barbecue on the Fourth of July. But Christmas was the most anticipated day of the year. Weeks before the celebration, parents and children gathered nuts and fruits; and the mothers sometimes sewed clothes with pieces of fabric they had accumulated during the year. Festivities might last for three to five days, and the fathers who lived on distant plantations came to visit their children. They brought homemade toys and sweets. On some plantations, the youngsters received candies, biscuits, oranges, popcorn, and some coins from their owner.

Musicians made fiddles with gourds, they covered their banjos with sheepskin, and they turned tree trunks and goatskins into drums. They created flutes with reed cane, hit frying pans with sticks, and stroked big bottles with the palm of their hand. With all these instruments, they played joyful music, and adults and children alike sang and danced all afternoon with pleasure.

At night, the children gathered around bonfires; they blew up hog bladders and popped them in the blaze like firecrackers.

Group Play

On large estates, there were plenty of friends to have fun with. Groups of children explored the windmills, sugar mills, tobacco houses, blacksmith shops, henhouses, barns, woods, rivers, and boat landings. They swam and played in the creeks where they sometimes held make-believe baptisms.

The children liked to play games like "anti-over" in which two teams stood on each side of a house, and one player threw a ball over the roof. The child who caught it on the other side ran around the building and tagged a player from the first team. Because the tagged player had to join the second team or be out, the children tried to avoid being tagged by running away. They also enjoyed playing traditional tag, and the girls jumped rope.

"Blindfold and Tag," "Peep Squirrel Peep," and "You Can't Catch Me" were popular hide-and-seek games. Being able to avoid detection was fun, but it was also a useful skill for children to learn. Those who later ran away from slavery could rely on their mastery in the art of hiding.

Children played circle games in which youngsters of all ages participated. One of the favorites was "Sail Away Rauley," in which children held hands and spun around faster and faster. Those who fell down were out of the game.

Toys

Since their parents had no or very little money, the children did not have much access to ready-made toys. They had to make their own, using their creativity and the material available on the plantations. They rolled up rags and held them together with string to

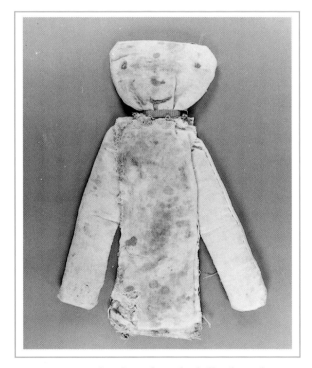

Young girls played with dolls that they created themselves using old rags. This example of a rag doll is from North Carolina.

form makeshift balls. A branch or a stick held between the legs became a horse. They fashioned stilts with tree limbs, and made little bows and arrows. They shot berries at one another through tubes of sugarcane. Girls played with dolls they created with rags, sticks, and cornhusks. One of the best-liked games was marbles. The children made them with clay hardened in the sun. When parents had succeeded in saving a little money by selling their produce or being hired out, they would buy inexpensive toys that the children were particularly proud of.

Slavery Games

Some of the games the children played had their origin in the particular situation of slavery. One was called "Warm Jacket." The children took a branch from a tree and struck their companions until their skin became hot. By getting used to the whip at an early age in a playful situation, the children were building their own defenses against the cruelty they would have to endure later.

Another sad game was "Auction Block." One child played the auctioneer and pretended he was selling his playmates to the highest bidder. The real auction block horrified the enslaved community because it separated the families. By playing auction, the children took some of the terror out of it. It was only a game, and at the end of the day they went back to their parents.

There were many deaths on the plantations due to overwork, hunger, savage whippings, and lack of care for the sick. Funerals were part of the children's world. One of their games was "Playing Church," during which they sang, prayed, and pretended to die. They also held mock funerals for small animals.

Black and White Children

The realities of plantation life also influenced other activities. During their free time, the children often came into contact with the white children who lived on the same estate. Some slaveholders and overseers forbade their children to play with the slave children, but others selected or even bought some youngsters to be their children's playmates.

Many people who grew up in slavery mentioned that they played freely with white children, and that they were good friends. Lunsford Lane stated: "I knew no difference between myself and the white children, nor did they seem to know any in turn."[3] Annie Burton confirmed this, recollecting fondly her

> care-free childhood days on the plantation, with my little white and black companions. . . . There were ten white children and fourteen colored children. Our days were spent roaming about from plantation to plantation, not knowing or caring what things [the Civil War] were going on in the great world outside our little realm.[4]

These good relations, unfortunately, did not last. The children were not to blame for the change, but their parents were. When the enslaved children started to work, the owners' children began to order them around and were pushed to do so by their parents. Pretty soon, the white companions of yesterday, imitating their mothers and fathers, treated their former playmates with disdain and cruelty.

They would use them as horses and whip them to make them go faster. When they played Indians and soldiers, the white children were the soldiers who won every battle and killed and scalped the Indians. During the Civil War, the slave children became the hated Yankees from the North captured by the triumphant Confederates of the South.

In many cases, white children ordered their enslaved companions to do things that were dangerous or forbidden. The children could not refuse to obey their owners' children and got beaten or whipped by the overseers or planters for disobeying the adults' orders. White parents also intervened quickly with slaps and lashes when they saw their children lose ground to the black children. John Jackson, of South Carolina, recalled that one day when he was about ten years old, he was digging hickory roots with his owner's son. Little John was faster and gathered more, which infuriated the white child, who kicked him in the nose. John wiped his blood on the other boy. The white boy's mother, John said, "whipped me on my naked back, to console her son, till the blood ran down."[5]

Sad and cruel as they were, such incidents were frequent because the slaveholders wanted to make sure that all the children, black and white, grew up understanding their future roles and places in society.

Chapter Five

Education for Life

Everything under slavery was conceived to make black people feel inferior and worthless. But, whether they were born in Africa or in America, they held a different opinion of themselves. They maintained their own traditions, values, and religious beliefs, and created others that they needed in order to cope with enslavement. Some of the lessons the people taught their offspring would have applied anywhere, but others could fit only the situation of enslaved children.

Lessons for Survival

Former slaves and slaveholders stressed that respect was important in the African-American community. As Frederick Douglass summed up, "There is not to be found, among any people, a more rigid enforcement of the law of respect to elders, than they maintain."[1] This deference to the elders was an African tradition, but it was also a way of keeping the community together. The adults were constantly humiliated and treated as children by the slaveholders, but they were, nonetheless, adults who had to be obeyed and considered. If parents had not instilled a very strong sense of respect in their children, the youngsters might have imitated the whites and dismissed and despised the adults. Such behavior would have destroyed the community.

Acting as kin, adults, whether parents or neighbors, had to steel children against appalling episodes that few people outside of slavery ever experienced. Some of the most difficult moments in the children's lives were to see their parents brutalized. Like adults, children were forced to watch when their companions or family members who had fought back or tried to run away were branded with hot irons on the face; had their ears, nose, or a foot cut off; or were whipped to death. The slaveholders thought that displays of terrible cruelty would frighten the rest of the community into obedience and submission.

The most common form of punishment was for grown men and women to be stripped naked in front of everyone and to receive dozens of lashes that cut their backs. It was an unbearable sight, especially for the children. William Wells Brown, a man who became a fugitive and a writer, remembered that when his mother got flogged, "the cold chills ran over me, and I wept aloud."[2] Many children attacked the men and women who whipped their parents. When Nelly, a mother of five, was dragged by the overseer to be whipped, Frederick Douglass recounted:

> three of [the children] were present, and though quite small, (from seven to ten years old, I should think) they gallantly came to their mother's defense, and gave the overseer an excellent pelting with stones. One of the little fellows ran up, seized the overseer by the leg and bit him.[3]

Some parents told their children they had to defend their family members, but most tried to prevent them from intervening because it was too dangerous.

In spite of the fact that slaves were expected to be submissive, many were not, and children sometimes saw their own parents or neighbors fight back. Nelly, for example, scratched and bit the overseer, and she cursed him even after she had received a severe flogging. This was not an isolated case, and such incidents inspired children. They saw how courageous some people were, and how they stood their ground, even though it could only bring them physical suffering and even death. The children were also aware that many adults and some children ran away to freedom. So they learned, by watching the different personalities in their community, that although the slaveholders presented submission as the only option for the people in bondage, these people could make other choices.

Even though they had witnessed and endured countless acts of savagery at an early age, the children, nevertheless, generally did not exhibit violence toward those weaker than they were or toward animals. The loving families and communities that gave them support and affection are certainly to be credited for this success.

Solidarity with the group was a necessity in order to survive, and the children were taught the importance of being united. Following the African tradition, children called people of their parents' age "uncle" and "aunt." Children their own age were called "brother" and "sister." This custom was extremely useful in America because the whole community truly acted as a family. When parents were sold away, the grandparents, aunts, uncles, siblings, or the rest of the community took charge of the children. The youngsters who had been sold and sent away were raised by the folks on the new plantation. The children born in Africa usually had no

The family was extremely important to enslaved people. Adults, made to feel worthless by their owners, saw the value of teaching respect for elders to their children. Following African tradition, children referred to all the adults around them as "uncle" or "aunt."

family in America, but they generally found adults willing to take care of them. Often, those foster parents were Africans who had been separated from their own children and welcomed the opportunity to raise other youths.

Discretion was a greatly valued quality that parents and the community instilled in the youngsters. The children learned at an early age never to repeat what they had heard or report what they had seen because it could bring punishment to their family and neighbors. Elijah P. Marrs explained that

> Mothers were necessarily compelled to be severe on their children to keep them from talking too much. Many a poor mother has been whipped nearly to death on account of their children telling white children things.[4]

Some parents, for example, stole food to feed their children; others hid people who had run away; still others made plans to flee or to revolt. Since the children could not fully understand these dangerous situations, their elders simply forbade them to report anything that was going on in the community.

Another useful tool for survival was handed down to the children: the art of concealment. Because a glance, gesture, smirk, or grimace could mean a flogging, or worse, it was vital for the children not to let the slaveholders see their displeasure, anger, or contempt. They learned to control their impulses and to display a happy face. As the fugitive Henry Watson explained:

> The slaveholder watches every move of the slave, and if he is downcast or sad,—in fact, if they are in any mood but laughing and singing . . . —they are said to have the devil in them.[5]

The slaveholders had decided early on that black people lacked intelligence and were thus suited to be slaves. Any demonstration to the contrary was a threat to the slave-holders' system. The enslaved population was well aware of the consequences it could suffer if it showed signs of clever-ness. Edward Walker, of Kentucky, recalled that he was better at arithmetic than his little white friend and his friend's father and uncle. When his owner realized that the boy was smart, he said Walker "had to be watched."[6] To avoid problems, the children learned to hide their intelligence and knowledge, and to play dumb when necessary. It was a terribly negative talent they had to develop in order to survive.

Learning to Read and Write

One type of knowledge it was often necessary to hide was the ability to read and write. All states vigorously discouraged literacy in the slave population because slaveholders thought that education would make people dissatisfied with their lot and prompt them to revolt. Their opinion was reinforced after Nat Turner's revolt in 1831, which caused the death of about sixty whites in Virginia, and in which literacy had played a role. In the late 1820s and 1830s, Virginia, Louisiana, North and South Carolina, and Georgia passed laws that banned the teaching of slaves and imposed fines, imprisonment, and whippings on the offenders. To frighten the slave community, the slaveholders circulated stories of people who had had their hands chopped off or were killed when seen writing. Although this was probably not true, there were actual cases of slave owners cutting a finger off the hands of literate slaves.

Some African children could already read and write when they arrived on the plantations. They were Muslim boys and girls who had studied Arabic in Qur'anic school. Arabic was not their mother tongue, but it was the language in which the Qur'an was written. By age thirteen, the good students could recite and sometimes write the major part of the book by memory. In America, the Muslims who wanted to maintain

While writing was forbidden by owners, and often by law, and schooling was not part of a slave's life, reading was sometimes acceptable, especially the reading of the Holy Bible. Some owners thought this would reinforce obedience.

their skills without pen and paper traced the words they had learned on the sand of the plantations.

For the vast majority of children growing up in slavery, formal education was impossible to get, but some managed to acquire the basics and others became quite literate. They usually started to study before they were eight, and by age ten or twelve, their education stopped, because they went to work full time. Some children were taught by their owners, who thought the slaves should have access to the Bible. The Holy Book, it was believed, would reinforce obedience in the slave population and acceptance of its fate in exchange for a better life in the hereafter.

Writing, on the other hand, was generally forbidden. The story of young John Warren explains why. He had learned to read but not to write, so he bought a bundle of letters from a white boy and taught himself to do so. Then John wrote passes allowing himself to travel, and he fled to Canada. Many men, women, and children did the same.

Some white children made a business of teaching their black acquaintances. Frederick Douglass gave bread to white boys in exchange for lessons. Other children offered the few pennies they made as apprentices to the white children willing to teach them. But some young whites were simply proud to teach or fond of their friends, and helped as much as they could until their parents intervened. The son of Edward Walker's owner started a class for his companions. His father reluctantly agreed, but when he discovered that Walker was learning fast, he made his son stop the classes after two weeks. In Mississippi, a group of white siblings taught John Crawford and five other slave children held by their father to read while hiding in a pine grove.

A small proportion of mulatto children received a good education in Northern boarding schools. The Healy brothers, who looked white, were sent by their Irish father to Quaker schools in the North. James, who was ordained in France, became the first Catholic priest and bishop of partly African origin in the United States; while Patrick served as president of Georgetown University. In Ohio, the school that became Wilberforce University had about two hundred mulatto children from the South in attendance during the 1850s.

NAT TURNER

Nat Turner was born in 1800 in Southampton, Virginia. His mother, who had been kidnapped from Africa, and his father taught Nat to read and write at an early age. Nat became a fugitive in his twenties, a few years after his father ran away. As Nat lived alone in the woods, he had a vision that he would lead a slave revolt. He then returned to the plantation to wait for the right time.

Turner became a preacher, and gathered followers and useful information as he traveled around the countryside. Finally, on August 22, 1831, he and about seventy companions launched the revolt he had envisioned. After three days, three thousand white men crushed the movement and killed more than one hundred people. Turner was captured a month later and hanged on November 11, 1831. His was the most deadly slave revolt in United States history, and far from gaining freedom for slaves, it led to even more brutality against the enslaved population, who, it was feared, might rise again.

Besides the help that some white people provided, many black children learned from African-American slaves. Their parents, older siblings, or another in the community taught them individually or held secret classes at night. It was an honored tradition for someone who could read and write to teach as many others as he or she could. Free African-Americans also helped. They had opened schools for their own sons and daughters and taught some slave children whose owners had allowed them to attend.

Children had often looked actively for whatever assistance they received when they sought literacy, and they displayed much ingenuity and perseverance in the pursuit of an education. Some youths were so eager to learn that they spent the little money they managed to make on books and writing supplies and devoted their limited leisure time to study. Richard Parker, of Virginia, picked up old nails and sold them until he had enough money to buy a spelling book that he hid under his hat. He continued to sell nails and bought marbles with his earnings. Each time he wanted to learn a letter, he gave a marble to a white boy. Benjamin Holmes, of South Carolina, studied the signs and names on the doors of the houses where he delivered bundles, and asked people to tell him a word or two at a time. Thomas Jones, of North Carolina, tried to buy a spelling book and was told that a slave should not try to read. He went to another store and said that a white boy had given him money and sent him on an errand to buy a book. With that trick, he got his spelling book.

The children who devoted their free time and energy to education knew that they were taking a lot of risks. Some were caught and had to suffer the consequences. When Richard Parker was discovered studying, he received fifteen blows. John Crawford and his five companions who studied with their white friends were whipped with a wooden paddle by the white boys' mother.

Many people who had been enslaved explained, when asked what had pushed them to learn how to read and write, that they wanted to better themselves. Some felt they were as good as the slaveholders, even though they were told that black people were not entirely human. They knew that if given a chance, they could do as well as anybody else. Learning to read and write was proof of their intellectual capacities. Others said they realized that if literacy was allowed to the whites and forbidden to the slaves, it must be good and useful.

Some of the children who dedicated themselves to learning did extremely well. One of the most renowned was Phillis Wheatley. She had been kidnapped in her native Senegal when only seven or eight years old and was enslaved in Boston in 1761. She may have gone to Qur'anic school and learned Arabic, because it was noted that soon after her arrival, she could be seen writing on walls with a piece of chalk or charcoal. Phillis learned English and Latin with her owner's children. She was such a good writer that a Rhode

Island newspaper published the young girl's poems when she was only fourteen. In 1773, at twenty, she published a book of thirty-nine poems in London, entitled *Poems on Various Subjects, Religious and Moral.* The first book published by an African-American woman, it was widely acclaimed in Europe and America. Phillis was freed the same year but died sick and poor in 1784.

Some of the Africans who had studied Arabic as children wrote letters, documents, and autobiographies in that language once in America. Job ben Solomon, enslaved in Maryland,

Written in Arabic, these are pages from a religious document authored by Bilali, originally from Guinea, while he was enslaved on a plantation in Georgia.

wrote a letter in Arabic to his father in Senegal, asking to be redeemed. He was freed in 1734 and sailed back home. One hundred years later, Ibrahima abd al-Rahman, the son of a famous ruler in Guinea, wrote a letter in Arabic. It was forwarded to the king of Morocco, who sought Ibrahima's release. After thirty-nine years of slavery in Mississippi, Ibrahima became free again in 1838; he returned to Africa with his wife. Other African scribes were Omar ibn Said, of Senegal, who wrote his autobiography in Arabic in 1831 in North Carolina; and Bilali, of Guinea, who produced a religious document in the 1830s from his plantation on Sapelo Island, Georgia. Many other Africans and African-Americans wrote autobiographies. They were the creators of a literary genre called Slave Narratives. These documents give us precious insights into the lives of the slave population and the plight of the children who grew up in slavery.

Chapter Six

In Search of Freedom

Few avenues existed for enslaved children to gain freedom. They could hope for their owner to emancipate them, or they could be purchased and then freed by members of their own family. Some children, however, took their fate in their own hands and ran away.

Getting their freedom back was very much on the minds of those taken from Africa, and bold and unafraid, many youngsters and adults escaped as soon as they set foot in the Americas. Freedom was a general preoccupation for all slave people, whether they were born free or had known nothing else but slavery.

During slavery, even young children had dreams of freedom. "From my earliest recollection freedom had been the object of my ambition, a constant motive to exertion, an ever-present stimulus to gain and to save," asserted Josiah Henson, a fugitive from Maryland who led a group of other escapees to liberty.[1] By the 1850s, more than 50,000 persons a year became runaways. Although most were taken back into slavery, tens of thousands successfully escaped to freedom before the Civil War. Children knew that freedom might be within their reach.

As Elijah P. Marrs recalled, "I had heard so much about freedom, and of colored people running off and going to Canada, that my mind was busy with this subject even in my young days."[2] But to gain their freedom, the children had to take enormous risks.

Running Away

The wish to run away came easily. The simple desire to be free, the dread of harsh punishments, and the longing for education were the principal reasons fugitives gave for their escape. But to actually flee was difficult. First, it meant leaving family, friends, or people who had helped and been kind and supportive. According to Frederick Douglass, many more people would have escaped from slavery if they had not been so closely bound to their families and friends. Some parents, however, actually encouraged their children to run away whenever they saw an opportunity. They knew that one person had a better chance at remaining undetected than a group, and so they encouraged their children to take that chance.

Four out of five fugitives were young men between the ages of fifteen and thirty. They were strong, resistant, and intrepid. Children under fifteen were willing to flee, and some succeeded in gaining their freedom, although they represented a small proportion of the fugitives. For example, on September 8, 1833, twelve-year-old Mary left the North Carolina estate of her owner. He thought she might be going to Hillsborough or Washington, where she knew people. Six months later, when she had not been found, he offered a reward of $25 for her capture.[3]

This painting, titled On to Liberty, *depicts a group of slaves running away during a battle of the Civil War, looking to use this opportunity to escape their grim lives.*

Once a youngster had decided to run away, there were many practical matters to take care of. Those who had learned to write had an advantage: They could forge a pass giving themselves permission to travel. Then, the future runaway had to gather some food for the trip. This was not an easy task since rations were small. Besides, stealing or hoarding food was dangerous and could make the slave owner suspicious. It was necessary to find some different clothes to take, because fugitive advertisements, which would be printed in newspapers or posted on trees and walls, described the clothing that people were wearing when they left. A change of clothes helped the runaways' chance of avoiding detection.

Next, they had to stash pepper. It was known that if pepper was sprinkled on the ground, bloodhounds used by slave-owners to chase runaways would lose their scent.

Once the preparations were complete, the future runaway had to wait for the right time to leave. The best day to do so was Saturday, because the overseer normally did not call on the workers until Monday morning. By that time, the escapee could already be a good distance away.

The big difficulty was to know where to go. Enslaved people very seldom left their plantation. They had little knowledge of its surrounding area, let alone what was a hundred miles away. But that did not deter numerous men, women, and children from escaping. For safety reasons, escapees had to stay away from the roads, clearings, and villages that would have made their travel easier. And even if they became lost, they could not ask for directions.

Besides freedom, another objective for those running away was to be reunited with relatives from whom they had been separated by sale. This was often the case with children. The escapees' destination was usually one of three types of places. Some chose to escape to a southern city where they could try to pass for free. Others joined Maroon communities, which were camps of fugitives hidden in forests and swamps. But in the nineteenth century, the majority of the escapees frequently wanted to reach the northern states that had already abolished slavery, or Canada West (later Ontario), where fugitives were declared free in 1793. When the rest of Canada abolished slavery in 1834, they tried to go there. After the Fugitive Slave Act was passed in 1850, the North did not seem safe to the runaways, who could be taken back to the South if discovered, so they therefore often attempted to take refuge in Canada. They walked by night toward the North Star for 600 to 1,000 miles (966 to 1,609 kilometers), in treks that could take anywhere from three months to a year. They knew they could find help and food in the slave quarters along the route, but they had to be alert and cautious in order not to endanger themselves and those who helped them.

The fugitive children learned to endure cold, hunger, thirst, loneliness, and fatigue as they walked for hundreds of miles. They had to conquer a normal fear of the unknown and of the wild animals and snakes that lived in the forests and swamps. But most of all, on their way to freedom, they had to fight their anxiety about being found by patrollers. They knew that if this happened, they could be torn up by vicious dogs especially bred for the hunting of fugitives. They would be brutally whipped when taken back to their plantation. Failure meant extreme punishment and, from then on, constant surveillance on the part of the overseer.

Most younger escapees did not go alone, but left with their families. Some of these groups traveled along what was known as the Underground Railroad. Very active between 1830 and 1865, the Underground Railroad was a network of several thousand people, both black and white, who provided help, shelter, and food to escapees. Harriet Tubman, herself a fugitive from Maryland, organized nineteen rescue missions to the South between 1850 and 1860, leading three hundred people, including children, along the Underground Railroad to freedom in the North and Canada.

Whatever form it took, escape demanded organization, courage, endurance, wit, adaptability, resourcefulness, and perseverance. The children had to take risks and assume responsibilities that were usually those of mature adults. Whether they failed and went back to slavery or succeeded and became free, they had demonstrated an intense commitment to freedom and a bravery seldom exhibited by anyone, child or adult.

The Price of Freedom

Some children did not have to go through the terrifying experience of running away. They were freed by their family. A man or a woman who had succeeded, at great cost, in buying his or her own freedom, generally did not stop there. Once free, the former slave worked steadily to earn as much money as possible. In contrast to white laborers, who could buy a farm or cattle with their savings and thus significantly improve their condition and that of their descendants, former slaves who had been freed or had bought their own freedom used their resources to purchase the freedom of their loved ones. They had children, parents, and siblings to liberate before they could even think of investing for the future. A whole lifetime could be spent buying one person at a time. Frank McWorter, for example, purchased himself, his wife, their thirteen children and two grandchildren for the huge sum, at the time, of $10,000. Mrs. Francis recalled that her mother had bought herself first for $650. Then she bought her daughter's freedom. "I was quite a strip of a girl before the sum was made up," Mrs. Francis said:

> On receiving my freedom, I went into the laundry to help my mother, and we worked and saved and denied ourselves everything until we had enough to purchase the freedom of my little brother.[4]

Next, they saved $1,200 and freed another sister. One of the most active emancipators was Aletheia Turner. She had been a slave of Thomas Jefferson and had bought her freedom. Over the next twenty-seven years, she purchased and liberated her sister, ten children, five grandchildren, two other women, and four other children. Black families of enslaved children had to pay dearly for their freedom, but white men who were the fathers of mulatto children had only to sign a paper to free their offspring.

Some children decided early that they were going to buy their own freedom. James Bradley had been kidnapped in Africa when he was only two years old. At fourteen, he spent his nights braiding corn husks to make horse collars. With the money the collars brought him, he bought pigs and cultivated corn at night to feed the animals. He also grew tobacco, which he sold to buy more grain for his pigs. Once fattened, he sold the hogs and bought some more. He also hired himself out to do odd jobs to make more money. The youngster was greatly overworked but, as he explained, "the hope of liberty strung my nerves, and braced up my soul so much, that I could do with very little sleep or rest."[5] After fourteen years of sacrifice and hard work, James Bradley was able to buy his freedom for $700.

The War and Emancipation

For the generation of children born in the 1850s, freedom came in 1865 without the risks of running away or the high cost of self-purchase. During the Civil War, however, they paid dearly in terms of insecurity, hunger, exploitation by the Union army, and slaveholders' retaliation.

The Emancipation Proclamation of 1863, which freed the slaves, was passed by the Union, but it was intended only for the states of the Confederacy. The states that remained within the Union, however, could legally maintain slavery. In the border states, those closest to the North—Maryland, Kentucky, Delaware, and Missouri—enslaved black men saw one opportunity for freedom: to run away and fight for the Union army. Between 40 and 60 percent of males deserted the plantations of the four border states and enlisted. Vengeful slaveholders who still retained the soldiers' families made the lives of their wives and children unbearable. These women and children were assigned the most strenuous jobs, severely beaten, or kicked off the plantations without any means of survival. And when they tried to take refuge with the Union army, they were turned away and told to go back to their owners.

RUMBLINGS OF WAR

The largely agricultural South wanted to preserve slavery and reopen the slave trade, since it relied heavily on slave labor to make its economy work. Southern leaders feared that as new states free of slavery entered the Union, the South would lose its influence in the government and be compelled to abolish slavery, which they believed would harm the economy of the South. To avoid this, the Southern states seceded from, or left, the Union, and the Civil War erupted in April 1861.

Meanwhile, in the Confederate states, more women and children ran away than ever before. Fugitives went from plantation to plantation to assemble the members of their family, and they fled together to Union army camps. The wives, children, and parents of the black men who had run away and enlisted in the Union army left their owners' estates and gathered on the outskirts of the military camps in the South, close to their male relatives. All these runaways were called "contraband of war" by the Union. Many of them were children, who suffered a great deal from inadequate food and shelter and lack of medical attention. In addition, their lives were made even more insecure by corrupt federal agents who sometimes sold them at a discount to the planters whose workers had left.

Some youngsters followed the grown men and enrolled in the Union army, where they served as laborers, soldiers, and drummers. Most got shoes and decent clothes for the first time in their lives. On the Confederate side, plantation owners turned soldiers did not want to renounce their comfort, so they took young slaves to the camps and battlefields to attend to their needs.

Free Children

The Thirteenth Amendment to the Constitution, which abolished slavery in 1865, did not mean automatic freedom

One way to gain freedom during the Civil War was to join the Union Army. This boy, barefoot and dressed in typical ragged clothes, ran away from his plantation and took refuge in an army camp.

for all the children of slavery. For example, apprenticeship laws were passed that allowed planters to keep thousands of free youths as involuntary laborers, until they were eighteen or twenty-one years of age, under slaverylike conditions. This situation was denounced by parents, who petitioned the authorities to recover their children, or took them from the plantations against the planters' will at great personal risk.

The people previously held in bondage did not celebrate emancipation only because they were technically free, but also because now they could reconstruct their families. For years after the Civil War, children and their relatives spent considerable time trying to locate one another. Because families had been separated by successive sales, it was a difficult task. A letter written in 1867 by Milly Johnson, of North Carolina, to the Freedmen's Bureau, established in 1865 to assist the newly freed people, lists the problems:

> It is my purpose to advertise for my children, When I last knew them they were 2 of them in Esics county VA, a girl and Boy, Living with their former owners. The Boy belonged to Hugh Billaps The Girl Belonged to Dr Richards. . . . There is another two a Girl and

Boy. They were sold to speculators [slave traders] at Richmond VA Where they were carried I do not Know. . . . There is still another Anna Johnson who is Living in Hertford Co., N.C. with Mr. Albert Elliott my former owner and since the surrender [the defeat of the Confederacy in the Civil War] he took her from me I protested against but to no avail.[6]

The dislocation of families was such that reunions were not numerous. Some people succeeded in finding a few relatives but could never locate others. Never-theless, people roamed the South in an attempt to find their loved ones. Former fugitives left Canada and the North to rejoin their children and spouses. Clearly, time and distance had not weakened the bonds that united black families.

With the abolition of slavery, it became possible for the newly freed to pursue knowledge openly. Several fugitives had mentioned that the desire to get an education was one of the reasons they fled their places of enslavement. Now, with freedom came the opportunity to read and write. Children and adults alike flocked to school. Booker T. Washington remembered that:

This picture shows the same boy after he became a drummer for the army. This was probably the first time he ever had shoes and decent, warm clothes. But many youngsters returned to slaverylike conditions after apprenticeship laws allowed plantation owners to keep them as involuntary laborers until they were eighteen or twenty-one years old.

After the abolition of slavery, many newly freed people rushed to attend school and pursue the knowledge they had been denied, including how to read and write. This school group consists of all children, but freed adults in large numbers also took advantage of what schooling they could.

it was a whole race trying to go to school. Few were too young, and none too old, to make the attempt to learn. As fast as any kind of teacher could be secured, not only were day-schools filled, but night-schools as well.[7]

Within a few years, large numbers of African-Americans could read and write.

Four million men, women, and children were now free, but they had no land, seeds, cattle, tools, or houses of their own. They had no compensation for years of unpaid labor. Some tried to live independently with their children by fishing, hunting, and cultivating land they had cleared. But laws were quickly passed that restricted their ability to do so successfully. Without economic independence, most freed adults and children were forced to continue working on the plantations for a share of the crops.

Freedom had come, but soon racist laws, known as Jim Crow laws, would enforce rigid segregation and overt discrimination in the South. The children who had grown up in slavery and experienced the hope and joy of freedom and political participation between 1865 and 1877, a time known as Reconstruction, found themselves living again in an oppressive, brutal world. Their own children would never know bondage, but they would not taste true freedom or equality.

As they became parents, the children of slavery drew on their painful experiences to shelter their offspring from the cruelty of racism, discrimination, and segregation. As they had done before, they had to find resources within themselves and their families and communities to cope with a disappointing and grim situation.

Most of the last generation of children who grew up in slavery lived and died poor and deprived of basic necessities. They endured the Great Depression of the 1930s, vicious racism, and, often, the indifference of the younger generations. Soon, books and movies would paint them in a distorted way that can still be seen today.

The children of slavery were far from being ignorant, easily scared, childlike, and naively happy, as books and films have portrayed them. On the contrary, they had learned to master the rules of a complex and dangerous world. They had been physically and mentally strong enough to successfully face abuse, racism, violence, injustice, hunger, overwork, separation from loved ones, and humiliation at an early age

Despite the horror of slavery and the hardships they endured even after freedom was gained, families and individuals persevered and continued to make important, profound contributions to the newly reunited nation.

and survive them all. They worked, helped one another, took risks, endured punishments, sought knowledge, and assumed responsibilities like the bravest adults. In addition, they succeeded in coming out of a harrowing experience without spreading hate, revenge, and violence. With resilience, they preserved their families and communities against terrible odds and built their own culture. Their abundant creativity gave America gifted poets, writers, inventors, musicians, painters, scholars, and orators.

The children who grew up in slavery were hardy survivors and unsung heroes.

Source Notes

INTRODUCTION

1. Cheryl Wright, *I Heard It Through the Grapevine: Oral Tradition in a Rural African-American Community in Brazoria, Texas.* Master's thesis, University of Houston, 1994, www.webarchaeology.com/html/cheroral.htm.

CHAPTER ONE

1. It is difficult to know exactly how many Africans were shipped to the Americas. The latest research suggests that the total number is more than 12 million and less than 20 million, and one study places it at 15.4 million. Joseph E. Inikori and Stanley L. Engerman, eds., *The Atlantic Slave Trade: Effects on Economies, Societies, and Peoples in Africa, the Americas, and Europe* (Durham: Duke University Press, 1992), p. 6.

2. Savannah Unit, Federal Writers Project, *Drums and Shadows: Survival Studies Among the Georgia Coastal Negroes* (Athens: The University of Georgia Press, 1940), p. 164.

3. Philip D. Curtin, ed. *Africa Remembered: Narratives by West Africans from the Era of the Slave Trade* (Madison: The University of Wisconsin Press, 1967), p. 301.

4. Allan D. Austin, ed. *African Muslim Slaves in Antebellum America: A Sourcebook* (New York: Garland, 1984), p. 623.

5. Edwards, ed. *Equiano's Travels* (London: Heinemann, 1969), p. 27.

6. Charles Ball, *Fifty Years in Chains 1837* (Reprint New York: Dover Publications, 1970), p. 186.

7. The United States abolished the slave trade from Africa in 1808. However, Africans continued to be shipped illegally. The last known slave ships to arrive in the United States were the *Clotilde* and the *Wanderer*, which landed in Alabama and Georgia in 1859, with a total of more than 550 Africans on board.

CHAPTER TWO

1. Thomas H. Jones, *The Experience of Thomas H. Jones, Who Was a Slave for Forty-three Years* (Boston: Bazin & Chandler, 1862), p. 6.
2. Jacob Stroyer, *My Life in the South* (Salem, MA: Salem Observer Books, 1885), p. 23.
3. Linda Brent (Harriet Jacobs), "Incidents in the Life of a Slave Girl," in *The Classic Slave Narratives*, Henry Louis Gates, ed. (New York: Mentor Books, 1987), p. 345.
4. Lewis Clarke, *Interesting Memoirs and Documents Relating to American Slavery, and the Glorious Struggle Now Making for Complete Emancipation* (London: Chapman Brothers, 1846) http://vi.uh.edu/pages/mintz/21.htm.
5. Bethany Veney, *The Narrative of Bethany Veney, a Slave Woman* (Worcester, 1889), p. 26.
6. Clarke.
7. Fredericka Bremer, *The Homes of the New World: Impressions of America* (London: A. Hall, Virtue, & Co., 1853), vol. 3: p. 10.
8. Moses Roper, *A Narrative of the Adventures and Escape of Moses Roper, from American Slavery* (Philadelphia: Merrihew & Gunn, 1838), p. 53.
9. Elizabeth Keckley, *Behind the Scenes, or Thirty Years a Slave, and Four Years in the White House* (New York: G. W. Carleton & Co., 1868), p. 28.
10. Moses Grandy, *Narrative of the Life of Moses Grandy: Late a Slave in the United States of America* (London: Gilpin, 1843), p. 8.
11. John W. Blassingame, *Slave Testimony: Two Centuries of Letters, Speeches, Interviews, and Autobiographies* (Baton Rouge: Louisiana State University, 1977), p. 396.
12. Ibid., p. 565.

CHAPTER THREE

1. Frances Anne Kemble, *Journal of a Residence on a Georgian Plantation in 1838–1839* (Athens: The University of Georgia Press, 1984), p. 229.
2. Annie L. Burton, *Memories of Childhood's Slavery Days* (Boston: Ross Publishing Company, 1909), p. 4.
3. Booker T. Washington, *Up from Slavery, An Autobiography* (New York: Bantam, 1967), p. 8.

4. Guy and Candy Carawan, *Ain't You Got a Right to the Tree of Life?* (Athens: The University of Georgia Press, 1989), p. 3.

5. John Michael Vlach, *Back of the Big House: The Architecture of Plantation Slavery* (Chapel Hill: The University of North Carolina Press, 1993), p. 162.

6. Jacob Stroyer, *My Life in the South* (Salem, MA: Salem Observer Books, 1885) p. 44.

7. Josiah Henson, *Father Henson's Story of His Own Life* (New York: J. P. Jewett, 1858), p. 18.

8. Ibid., p. 43.

9. John W. Blassingame, *Slave Testimony: Two Centuries of Letters, Speeches, Interviews, and Autobiographies* (Baton Rouge: Louisiana State University, 1977), p. 49.

10. John Andrew Jackson, *The Experience of a Slave in South Carolina* (London: Passmore & Alabaster, 1862), p. 23.

CHAPTER FOUR

1. Bouki is the name of the hyena in the folktales of Senegal, West Africa. Senegalese people brought those tales with them when they were shipped to America during slavery.

2. Ronald Killion, *Slavery Time When I Was Chillun Down on Marster's Plantation* (Savannah: Beehive Press, 1973), p. 25.

3. Lunsford Lane, *The Narrative of Lunsford Lane* (Boston, 1842), p. 6.

4. Annie L. Burton, *Memories of Childhood's Slavery Days* (Boston: Rose Publishing Company, 1909), p. 3.

5. John Andrew Jackson, *The Experience of a Slave in South Carolina* (London: Passmore & Alabaster, 1862), p. 7.

CHAPTER FIVE

1. Frederick Douglass, *My Bondage and My Freedom 1855* (New York: Dover Publications, 1969), p. 69.

2. William Wells Brown, *Narrative of William W. Brown, A Fugitive Slave* (Boston: Anti-Slavery Office, 1847), p. 16.

3. Douglass, p. 93.

4. Elijah P. Marrs, *Life and History* (Louisville, 1855), p. 11.

5. Henry Watson, *Narrative of Henry Watson, A Fugitive Slave* (Boston, 1848), p. 32.

6. John W. Blassingame, *Slave Testimony: Two Centuries of Letters, Speeches, Interviews, and Autobiographies* (Baton Rouge: Louisiana State University, 1977), p. 517.

CHAPTER SIX

1. Josiah Henson, *Father Henson's Story of His Own Life* (New York: J.P. Jewett, 1858), p. 25.
2. Elijah P. Marrs, *Life and History* (Louisville, 1855), p. 12.
3. Fayetteville *Observer*, March 14, 1834.
4. John W. Blassingame, *Slave Testimony: Two Centuries of Letters, Speeches, Interviews, and Autobiographies* (Baton Rouge: Louisiana State University, 1977), p. 509.
5. Ibid., p. 688.
6. Ira Berlin and Leslie S. Rowland, eds. *Families and Freedom: A Documentary History of African-American Kinship in the Civil War Era* (New York: The New Press, 1997), p. 215.
7. Booker T. Washington, *Up from Slavery, An Autobiography* (New York: Bantam, 1967), pp. 20–21.

Bibliography

Ball, Charles. *Fifty Years in Chains, 1837.* Reprint New York: Dover Publications, 1970.

Berlin, Ira, and S. Leslie Rowland, eds. *Families and Freedom: A Documentary History of African-American Kinship in the Civil War Era.* New York: The New Press, 1997.

Blassingame, John W., ed. *Slave Testimonies: Two Centuries of Letters, Speeches, Interviews, and Autobiographies.* Baton Rouge: Louisiana State University, 1977.

Botkin, B. A., ed. *Lay My Burden Down: A Folk History of Slavery.* Chicago: The University of Chicago Press, 1945.

Bremer, Fredericka. *The Homes of the New World: Impressions of America.* London: A. Hall, Virtue & Co., 1853.

Brown, William Wells. *Narrative of William W. Brown, a Fugitive Slave.* Boston: Anti-Slavery Office, 1847.

Burton, Annie L. *Memories of Childhood's Slavery Days.* Boston: Ross Publishing Company, 1909.

Carawan, Guy and Candy. *Ain't You Got a Right to the Tree of Life?* Athens: The University of Georgia Press, 1989.

Clarke, Lewis. *Interesting Memoirs and Documents Relating to American Slavery, and the Glorious Struggle Now Making for Complete Emancipation.* London: Chapman Brothers, 1846.

Curtin, Philip, ed. *Africa Remembered: Narratives by West Africans from the Era of the Slave Trade.* Madison: The University of Wisconsin Press, 1967.

Diouf, Sylviane. *Servants of Allah: African Muslims Enslaved in the Americas.* New York: New York University Press, 1998.

Douglass, Frederick. *My Bondage and My Freedom, 1855.* Reprint New York: Dover Publications, 1969.

Gates, Henry Louis, ed. *The Classic Slave Narratives.* New York: A Mentor Book, 1987.

Grandy, Moses. *Narrative of the Life of Moses Grandy: Late a Slave in the United States of America.* London: Gilpin, 1843.

Henson, Josiah. *The Life of Josiah Henson, Formerly a Slave Now An Inhabitant of Canada. Narrated by Himself.* Boston: A.D. Phelps, 1849.

———. *Father Henson's Story of His Own Life.* New York: J.P. Jewett, 1858.

Jackson, John Andrew. *The Experience of a Slave in South Carolina.* London: Passmore & Alabaster, 1862.

Jones, Thomas H. *The Experience of Thomas H. Jones Who Was a Slave for Forty-three Years.* Boston: Bazin & Chandler, 1862.

Keckley, Elizabeth. *Behind the Scenes, or Thirty Years a Slave, and Four Years in the White House.* New York: G.W. Carleton & Co., 1868.

Kemble, Frances Anne. *Journal of a Residence on a Georgian Plantation in 1838–1839.* Athens: The University of Georgia Press, 1984.

Killion, Ronald. *Slavery Time When I Was Chillun Down on Marster's Plantation.* Savannah: Beehive Press, 1973.

King, Wilma. *Stolen Childhood: Slave Youth in Nineteenth-Century America.* Bloomington: Indiana University Press, 1995.

Lane, Lunsford. *The Narrative of Lunsford Lane.* Boston, 1842.

Marrs, Elijah P. *Life and History.* Louisville, 1885.

Mellon, James, ed. *Bullwhip Days: The Slaves Remember.* New York: Avon Books, 1988.

Roper, Moses. *A Narrative of the Adventures and Escapes of Moses Roper, from American Slavery.* Philadelphia: Merrihew & Gunn, 1838.

Savannah Unit, Georgia Writers' Project, WPA. *Drums and Shadows: Survival Studies Among the Georgia Coastal Negroes.* Athens: The University of Georgia Press, 1986.

Stroyer, Jacob. *My Life in the South.* Salem: Salem Observer Books, 1885.

Veney, Bethany. *The Narrative of Bethany Veney, a Slave Woman.* Worcester, 1889.

Washington, Booker T. *Up from Slavery, an Autobiography.* Reprint New York: Bantam, 1967.

Watson, Henry. *Narrative of Henry Watson, A Fugitive Slave.* Boston, 1848.

Wright, Cheryl. *I Heard It Through the Grapevine: Oral Tradition in a Rural African American Community in Brazoria, Texas.* Master's Thesis University of Houston, 1994.

To Learn More

A Selection of Books, Web Sites, and Videos

AFRICA

Books

Brooks, Larry. *Daily Life in Ancient and Modern Timbuktu*. Minneapolis: Runestone, 1999.

Diouf, Sylviane A. *Kings and Queens of Africa*. New York: Franklin Watts, 2000.

Minks, Louise. *Traditional Africa*. San Diego: Lucent Books, 1996.

Ofosu-Appiah, L. H. *People in Bondage: African Slavery in the Modern Era*. Minneapolis: Runestone, 1993.

Web Sites

www.edunetconnect.com/cat/timemachine/index.html (A look at what has happened in Africa and the rest of the world from 25 to 10,000 years ago)

www.campus.northpark.edu/history/WebChron/Africa/ (A timeline of Africa south of the Sahara)

Video

Dark Passages. (Documents the Atlantic slave trade) PBS, 1990.

SLAVE NARRATIVES AND BIOGRAPHIES

Books

Ball, Charles, Jane Shuter, eds. *Charles Ball and American Slavery*. Raintree Steck–Vaughn Publishers, 1995.

Burns, Bree. *Harriet Tubman*. Philadelphia: Chelsea House, 1994.

Douglass, Frederick. *Escape from Slavery: The Boyhood of Frederick Douglass in His Own Words*. New York: Knopf, 1994.

Equiano, Olaudah. *The Kidnapped Prince: The Life of Olaudah Equiano*. New York: Knopf, 1994.

Fleischner, Jennifer. *I Was Born a Slave: The Story of Harriet Jacobs*. Brookfield: The Millbrook Press, 1997.

McKissack, Patricia. *A Picture of Freedom: The Diary of Clotee, a Slave Girl*. New York: Scholastic, 1997.

Myers, Walter Dean. *Amistad: A Long Road to Freedom*. New York: Dutton, 1998.

Rinaldi, Ann. *Hang a Thousand Trees with Ribbons: The Story of Phillis Wheatley*. San Diego: Harcourt Brace, 1996.

Young, Mary and Gerald Horne. *Testaments of Courage: Selections from Men's Slave Narratives*. New York: Franklin Watts, 1995.

Web Sites

www.metalab.unc.edu/docsouth (Original slave narratives in their entirety)

http://vi.uh.edu/pages/mintz/primary.htm (Excerpts from early travel narratives of Europeans to Africa and from slave narratives)

www.uncg.ed/~jpbrewer/remember (Audio interviews of former slaves, collected in the 1940s)

www.amistad.mysticseaport.org (The *Amistad* story with biographies of some of the Africans)

Videos

A Woman Called Moses. (Harriet Tubman). Xenon Entertainment, 1978.

Booker. (Booker T. Washington). Bonneville Worldwide Entertainment, 1984.

Frederick Douglass: An American Life. Valencia Entertainment Corporation, 1985.

Solomon Northup's Odyssey (The life of a free man kidnapped into slavery). Monterey Home Video, 1984.

HISTORY OF AFRICAN AMERICANS AND SLAVERY

Books

Hamilton, Virginia. *Many Thousand Gone: African Americans from Slavery to Freedom*. New York: Knopf, 1995.

Haskins, Jim. *Black, Blue and Gray: African-Americans in the Civil War*. New York: Simon & Schuster, 1998.

Nardo, Don. *Braving the New World: From the Arrival of the Enslaved Africans to the American Revolution, 1619–1784*. Philadelphia: Chelsea House, 1995.

Palmer, Colin. *The First Passage: Blacks in the Americas 1520–1617*. New York: Oxford University Press, 1995.

Paulson, Timothy. *Days of Sorrow, Years of Glory: From the Nat Turner Revolt to the Fugitive Slave Law, 1831–1850*. Philadelphia: Chelsea House, 1994.

Wood, Peter. *Strange New Land: African Americans, 1617–1776*. New York: Oxford University Press, 1996.

Web Sites

www.toptags.com/aama (This very informative site contains historical documents, biographies, electronic books, speeches, folktales, and trivia games)

www.geocities.com:80/Athens/forum/9061/afro/afro/html (African-American history, arts, and literature)

www.pbs.org/wgbh/aia (Public Television's acclaimed series *Africans in America*)

www.lcweb.loc.gov/exhibits/african (A Library of Congress exhibit on African-American history)

Videos

The Autobiography of Miss Jane Pitman (Fictional account of the life of a 110-year-old former slave from the Civil War to the civil rights era). Prism Entertainment, 1974.

The Massachusetts 54th Colored Infantry (An African-American regiment during and after the Civil War). PBS video, 1994.

LITERACY

Book

Burchard, Peter. *Charlotte Forten: A Black Teacher in the Civil War.* New York: Crown Publishers, 1995.

Videos

Charlotte Forten's Mission. Monterey Home Video, 1985.
Nightjohn. (A slave teaches a young girl how to read.) Hallmark Home Entertainment, 1996.

THE UNDERGROUND RAILROAD

Book

Gorrell, Gena K. *North Star to Freedom: The Story of the Underground Railroad.* New York: Delacorte Press, 1997.

Web Sites

www.nationalgeographic.com/features/99/railroad (An interactive exploration)
www.cr.nps.gov/aahistory (African-American historical sites, including the Underground Railroad, by the National Park Service)

Videos

Follow the Drinking Gourd. (A family escapes to freedom)
Roots of Resistance: A Story of the Underground Railroad. PBS video, 1989.

Genealogies

Look for ancestors who grew up in slavery.
www.freedmensbureau.com
www.prairiebluff.com/aacensus

Index